All

Kay Bascom

OlivePress
צהר זית

HE FULFILLED ALL, HE DESERVES OUR ALL

ALL

*And beginning with Moses and
all the Prophets, He explained to them
what was said in all the Scriptures
concerning Himself. Luke 24:27*

Kay Bascom

OlivePress
צהר זית

ALL HE FULFILLED ALL, HE DESERVES OUR ALL

ISBN 978-1-941173-29-9

A *Messiah Mystery* Resources publication

Published in the USA

Published by

Olive Press Messianic and Christian Publisher
www.olivepresspublisher.org
olivepressbooks@gmail.com

Cover background images from Bing.com/images

Our prayer at Olive Press is that we may help make the Word of Adonai fully known, that it spread rapidly and be glorified everywhere. We hope our books help open people's eyes so they will turn from darkness to Light and from the power of the adversary to God and to trust in ישוע Yeshua (Jesus). (From II Thess. 3:1; Col. 1:25; Acts 26:18,15 NRSV *New Revised Standard Version* and CJB, the Complete Jewish Bible.)

The author's website: www.messiahmysteryresources.org

*He said to them, "How foolish you are, and how slow [of heart] to believe **ALL** that the prophets have spoken! Did not the Messiah have to suffer these things and then enter his glory?" And beginning with Moses and **ALL** the Prophets, he explained to them what was said in **ALL** the Scriptures concerning himself.*

LUKE 24:25-27 (NIV 2011)

Table of Contents

INTRODUCTION

We live in perilous and confused times. The signs of the times are converging quickly along Biblical lines. Although it is hard to "see the forest for the trees," consider these broad entities: wars escalating, martyrs multiplying, refugees fleeing, nature groaning, economies collapsing, digitalization escalating, Israel surrounded, the West reneging its support for the Middle East's only democracy. Yet there are encouraging signs — Jewish Diaspora regathering, Messianic believers rising, third-world leadership maturing, and the world's tribes and peoples being ever more widely reached.

In such tense times, believers sorely need an informed grasp and deep experience of who God says our Lord is. It is in the Old Testament that God has given us the foundation of our faith. That is where the story of redemption begins. God's Word lays the groundwork for us to understand how wonderfully the Messiah He sent meets our every need, for as *ALL* presents, He is God's ultimate Seed, His Son, His Lamb, His Priest, His Feasts' Host, His King, and His ultimate Prophet. Humanity's needs introduced in the Old Testament are met by the Messiah who died and rose to save us. It is He who declared the Old Testament was all about Himself (Luke 24:25-27).

Why is an Old Testament-based study of the broad story of redemption like *ALL* important today? Because its lack is dangerous. We need firm grounding and joyful confidence in our Lord. We may be called upon to face unprecedented challenges to faith in the Lord Jesus, the Christ — *Yeshua ha Mashiach*, as He was called during the Incarnation. Why? Because we may be caught asleep as another Holocaust is developing. We need to be well-equipped with truth and the spiritual weapons of our warfare at such a time as this. We would be wise to prepare our own minds and hearts for martyrdom.

We find ourselves in a world that is progressively rejecting and marginalizing Christianity, and one that is ever-more hostile toward the God of Abraham, Isaac, and Jacob. Jews, Israel, "chosen people," Christians, anyone claiming divine calling — they are anathema to proudly independent man, secularized man, globalized man, Caliphate man, Adamic man. Satan has used these tactics for centuries, and is enjoying their escalation in today's violent, narcissistic, and media-controlled world.

Meanwhile the Church is not only under fire from without but is infected from within. Biblical truths revealed in God's Word are rampantly being twisted, rewritten, or denied. This is not new. Christendom has inherited the results of centuries of deviation from Biblical truth and related broken relationships. The New Testament introduces a whole new Covenant, one including world-wide "branches," grafted into the old Covenant Jewish "root." Yet a litany of quotations from early Gentile Church fathers exposes interpretations and attitudes that have led to centuries of humiliation, alienation, exile, persecution, and genocidal attacks upon Jews. Scriptural deterrents to such attitudes were violated and ignored. This tragic situation grew out of false doctrines which are today called "Replacement Theology." (*See the Appendix for resources critiquing this unfortunate legacy absorbed by many Christian denominations.*) In these perilous times, the Body of Christ urgently needs to get back to Biblical truth and right relationships among all believers in the God of Abraham, Isaac, and Jacob.

Recently in the estrangement gap between Jewish and Gentile communities a spreading movement is rising that hearkens back to the times of the Incarnation. Israel's "tree" is beginning to bud again! (See Romans 11:24, Matthew 24:32.) Note two signs of this new era. First, Israel is relocated in the Promised Land after a two-thousand year absence. Secondly, whole communities of Jewish believers in *Yeshua* are emerging in Israel, America, and beyond. They are proclaiming that Jesus *(Yeshua)* actually was and is Israel's true Messiah!

This "budding" comes as a shock both to Jewish people and to the Church. After centuries of un-corrected relationships between Jews and Gentiles, the Reformation failed to deal with this festering illness. Jews faced genocidal attack in Europe, yes, in the very heart of Luther's "Christian" Germany. How can the Jewish community see anything "Christian" as good? However, the rise of the Messianic Movement — Jewish believers in *Yeshua* the Messiah — is beginning to challenge long-held resentments, theologies, and prejudices in both faith communities.

The Church finds this new situation befuddling. Having been Gentilized in the early centuries, Christendom is now faced with an authentic community that was envisioned in Scripture: "one new man" (Ephesians 2:15) consisting of two distinct identities. These identities have been pitted against one another over the centuries due to the deceitful but very effective work of the enemy of God and man. The emergence of today's Messianic movement is now spotlighting this blight on God's people — two peoples — "root" and "branch" people. It exposes the failure of the grafted-in wild Gentile "branches" to heed Scripture's warning not to boast over the "root" (Romans 9:13-24) — the natural "olive tree." It also recognizes the Savior's identity, which Israel's leadership missed.

ALL attempts to take the reader back to the Biblical foundations of God's plan to redeem humanity and restore His world. It calls attention to the Gentilized Scriptural interpretation which "spiritualizes" the Old Testament rather than considering its teachings in a straightforward manner. This has effectively marginalized study of the Old Testament, undercutting its significance to today's Christians. *ALL* yearns to reverse the relational malpractice which the Church has inherited due to centuries of a Replacement Theology that has taught that Israel is finished and has been replaced by the Church as God's chosen people, having become "the New Israel." How very presumptuous, how very wrong, how very blind to God's continual affirmation of His undying love for the people He sovereignly chose for giving the world His Scriptures and His Messiah! How dismissal of the prophets' assurances of Israel's eventual restoration. How imbedded in history the Holocaust was, and how alive is its spirit in our world today.

Awake, Israel and the Church! Be reconciled, restored, and renewed! May God's unfailing love felt by Paul (Romans 9:4-5) find a home in our hearts:

> *"Theirs is the adoption as sons; theirs the divine glory, the covenants, the receiving of the law, the temple worship and the promises. Theirs are the patriarchs, and from them is traced the human ancestry of the Messiah, who is God over all, forever praised! Amen."* (NIV 2011)

Ω

STUDY SUGGESTIONS

Welcome to this quest for the person of the Messiah throughout the Old Testament! Yes, *the Old Testament* is full of Him, even as He told the travelers on the Emmaus Road the Sunday night after Jesus' resurrection. He chided them for being "slow of heart to believe all that the prophets have spoken." He opened the Scriptures to them that night recorded in Luke 24. "Beginning with Moses and *all* the Prophets he explained to them what was said in *all* the Scriptures concerning himself."

"All" would have been marvelous to hear from the risen Son Himself! As we look at His disciples' accounts in the Gospels and Acts, we realize they were informed by what Jesus was telling them when He was on earth, and what His Spirit was showing to them, thereafter. This study called *ALL* is an attempt to briefly bring into focus some glimpses of the Messiah that were sprinkled all through the Old Testament. The Old Testament *fills full* the fulfillments recorded in the New Testament!

Study suggestions: Since *ALL* is a panoramic overview of the Old Testament in just a few short lessons, it becomes an unusual undertaking. The time investment can yield various kinds of fruit:

➢ **Focus**: (Revelation 22:13a) *"I am the Alpha and the Omega."* The Messiah is our compass, road map, and dynamic for the Biblical pilgrimage.

➢ **Fellowship:** (Matthew 18:20) *"For where two or three come together in my name, there I am with them."* We meet Him as we study in community.

➢ **Faithfulness:** (Matthew 6:33). *"But seek first his kingdom and his righteousness, and all these things will be given to you as well."* He clarifies our priorities.

➢ **Awakening**: (Luke 24:27). *"...he explained to them what was said in all the scriptures concerning Himself." We hear the risen Lord Jesus speak.*

➤ **Application**: (II Timothy 3:16 KJV) "All scripture is given by inspiration of God and is profitable for doctrine, for reproof, for correction, for instruction in righteousness." *God enlists our cooperative openness and obedience.*

The adventure: How many references are investigated, how earnest the accompanying prayer, how serious the engagement with implications – these will vary from group to group and person to person. None of this can happen without the work of the Holy Spirit, on whom we depend for the process and the results.

Suggestions for leaders:

1. Shepherding: Be responsive to your group, tailoring your format to their needs, and praying regularly for each of them.

2. Timing: Some groups may wish to alter the twelve-week timing, lingering longer on some studies, or all. Study 6 is a parenthetical resource that could be amplified, and could well be given extra time.

3. Method: Help the class *be present to Jesus* when He appears in Scripture. Each person can identify with a character in the passage, and then react to Jesus. *Feel* the scene with all five senses, plus the heart.

4. The real Teacher: Depend on the Holy Spirit to reveal the Lord Jesus, so that hearts and lives will be changed, to the glory of God the Father.

5. Attitude: Enjoy this pilgrimage with our loving Lord!

6. Resources: *The Messiah Mystery* and *Keys to the Messiah Mystery* are study aids by the same author which the leader may use that match the themes of *ALL* and its companion studies, *In* and *Therefore.*

7. Goal: Help the group realize that transformation, not information, is our goal. A kick-off or wrap-up focus for each study might be:

    "How does knowing Jesus as your Second Adam (or Lamb, Priest, Host, Prophet, King) impact your life?"

    May you be deeply blessed, dear Reader.

    Kay Bascom

Study I

QUEST

What, Why, How, When, Where, Who?

WELCOME TO A LOOK AT LIFE'S SUPREME QUEST!
Below are some questions that are natural to ask.

WHAT? The subject of *ALL* throughout every chapter is the identity and meaning of the Messiah. This mystery was of necessity concealed in the Old Testament, but meticulously disclosed in the New. The Incarnation of the Son of man marked the historical moment when this mystery was unveiled. Next, the arrival of the Holy Spirit on earth marked the spiritual moment-of-truth when the power of the mystery was set loose in the world to continue the Incarnation.

WHY? We live today in a sound-bite world, a world that is losing the continuity between cause and effect. History is being discarded or re-written according to the fad of the day. The story of the relationship between God and man is of profound importance. The Bible is the one source of that history. Missing God's message is unnecessary in a literate society, and we put ourselves at risk in a shortsighted, uninformed, unredeemed state of living, when we reject or ignore "the manual for humanity" given us by God. History (His story) happened progressively, but the account is gathered together under one cover. The central figure is the Messiah. People who claim to "know" Him say that knowing Him in a living way is the most important quest in life. *For personal reflection:*

Do I know Him in a living way?

Would I want to if that were possible?

HOW? This method is "panoramic." Tackling the Bible as a whole may seem daunting, but it is a wise choice to make for anyone serious about life's pilgrimage. Even though various area maps are crucial, an overview of the road system along a whole route gives a sense of direction to a traveler who wants to reach a destination. Getting a sense of the whole message of the Bible can immensely enhance understanding the parts. Various types of Bible study — of books, characters, periods, subjects, and words — are all enriched and unified by getting a sense of where they fit into the whole. We need both the telescope and the microscope to study God's physical creation; we need those perspectives to enjoy His spiritual creation fully, too.

For private assessment:

How clear or hazy is my overview of the history of the human race, i.e., the message of the Bible?

WHEN? Knowing when something happened along the story line of salvation history clarifies and deepens its meaning. Getting a view from the vantage point of both Time and Eternity can free us up to think "outside the box." *ALL* helps you look down from God's perspective. Scripture speaks of life as a great race with a goal and spectators and issues that matter.

Do I have an orientation to what I have been born into, from the stand point of both Time and Eternity?

WHERE? Getting a sense of where we are today in this great story is a reasonable quest. While devotional application of short sections of Scripture is vital for the individual, we also need to have an awareness of a passage's meaning when written, its challenge for the present, and its promise of hope for the future.

Discussion Question: If we are living somewhere along the continuum of man's pilgrimage in relationship to his Maker, does it make any difference to us where we are today on that line? Why?

WHO ME? We are not machines. Humans are personal. The answer to our life quest must be personal. A Bible study may be done with a group, but its assets are tied up in the personal quest of each member. This would be a good time to check your own responses to the *ALL* invitation, and consider these issues. After you have thought about this privately, maybe you would be willing to share some of your responses, or at least listen to someone else's in the group. Here are some issues to reflect on, or discuss:

✓ How interested are you in a Biblically based study? Much, little, tolerable, curious, or what?

✓ And why? (Am I a searcher... bored...spiritually over-stuffed? What makes me eager, or not, to engage?)

✓ Do you think of humanity's life, or your own life, as a race in any sense? Would you like to bear "a Lighted Baton"?

✓ Would you like to think outside of Time, and get God's perspective?

✓ When does being human (caught in Time's limitations) frustrate you?

✓ How do you respond to life's most unavoidable fact: death? To you, is death painful, frightening, avoided, too far off to care about, or what? Is a way out of death important to you?

ALL **WORDING ORIENTATION: "Messiah" is used for "Christ"** repeatedly in this study. Both words mean "the Anointed One." "Messiah" (Hebrew derivation) has deep Old Testament roots, and points toward a figure long expected in Old Covenant times. The term "Christ" is the same word but comes from a Greek derivation. "Christ" is more universalized, less "Jewish." It reflects less background from the past and expectation for the future. To stress the inter-relatedness of both the Old and New Testaments, "Messiah" is more often used in *ALL* . Occasionally Jesus' Hebrew name, *Yeshua*, will be used when during His Incarnation, to alert us to His Jewishness.

New Testament examples of "Messiah" used by Jews or Samaritans trained in the Old Testament Scriptures:
John 1:41
John 4:25

The 2011 NIV translation of the angel's message to the shepherds uses "Messiah." The 1984 version says "or Messiah" in the footnote.
Luke 2:11

"SHADOW AND SUBSTANCE" refers to the Messiah's appearance in "shadows" in Old Testament times, then in "substance," or reality, at the Incarnation. We who live today have the Old Testament and the New as well. We know about the later events of the Incarnation, the Cross, and the Resurrection. In the Gospels and Letters, the early believers passed on how the Spirit of God taught them to interpret God's eternal plan. The Scriptures move from the Old Covenant to the New — from early "shadows" to the Incarnation's substance — from the hidden "types" to the realities – from "copies" to originals – i.e., from predictions to fulfillment. Examples of this "shadow and substance" terminology:

Colossians 2:17

Hebrews 8:5

Hebrews 10:1

WHY ARE SO MANY SCRIPTURE REFERENCES GIVEN IN *ALL*? Although many readers will not take time to look up these many references, their presence grounds the study in Biblical truth. They provide a quick way to check the source behind an allegation. Depth of scriptural engagement will vary. The Bereans in Acts 17:11 were called "noble"…"for they received the message with great eagerness and examined the Scriptures every day to see if what Paul said was true."

A NOTE ON CAPITALIZATION: The author regrets the text's distracting inconsistency when it comes to capitalization of pronouns referring to deity. Unfortunately the NIV version (like many versions) does not capitalize them. If the author uses caps (so basic to my thinking) and the Bible quote does not, a variation occurs every time Scripture is printed. Quotations from other works involve this mixture of treatment, as well, yet they must be quoted as originally written. Apologies!

SYMBOL SHORTCUTS: To indicate the path of historical progression, symbols introduce some sections of the *ALL* studies. To simplify, the order of study will roughly trace each chapter's theme in sequence from 1 to 5, as shown in the following chart.

1: ⇐ Old Testament events.

2: ⇓ Incarnation events.

3: ⇒ the Spirit's illumination in the New Testament record.

4: ↓ new disclosures from heaven in the Book of Revelation.

5: ♥ This symbolizes our mind/will response via the heart.

⇐	⇓	⇒	↓	♥
Before: BC	**INCARNATION**	After: AD	About 90 AD	Now:
"shadow" O.T. "type"	"substance" N.T. reality	Holy Spirit's illumination	Revelation from heaven	My own response
I Cor. 10:11	Phil. 2:6-8	John 16:12-15	Rev. 1:1-2	I Tim. 1:5

So the panoramic flow (symbolized above) goes from pre-history, to the Cosmic Event, to the results of and revelations about that Event, to my own personal response. (How will the Event happen to/in me?)

Other markings used:

⇔ This symbol indicates both Testaments, so points both ways.

✹ This stands for something quite new or especially amazing.

☞ This marks a verse to be memorized as the chapter's key thought.

WE ARE FELLOW PILGRIMS DURING OUR LAP ON EARTH. For perspective on life's pilgrimage, discuss Hebrews 12:1-13.

Who do you think the "great cloud of witnesses" refers to?

Who is in the race?

What is its goal?

♥ **A RACE CAN BE DIFFICULT**, but in life, we'll cover the course one way or another. Look at the promise for earnest "racers" in Isaiah 40:31.

Would you like to claim it?

What would your part in the process be?

About prayer: *Since this ALL attempt at looking at life's pilgrimage is impossible without our Divine Teacher's help, the starting place for our search is to ask for the illumination of the Holy Spirit! That is His ministry and His delight.*

Ω

Study 2

WHO

What is life's great identity quest?

Introduction: This *ALL* study is basically an examination of the **credentials of a Claimant**. He either did accomplish a reversal of death or else he didn't. He either is the author of eternal life or he isn't. The stakes are high—deliverance or despair. Each of us faces God alone, minus our "clique" or "generation." Each of us has evidence to examine, and a choice to make.

Today's society is infected with a culture of death. Death threatens, fascinates, and cuts off life. Death is the crux of Shakespearean and modern tragedies, the weapon of nations, the tool of the powerful, the threat of nature, and the dread of illness. For the cynic drowned in existentialism, dramatic death is a means for self-authentication. Jihad "suicide" is even celebrated in one religion as the assured route to reward in Paradise. Where did death come from? The first chapters of Genesis give us a record of how death came into the world, and what action the Creator took to reverse its effects. That is what the term "Good News" is about.

God speaks from Eternity into Time. He speaks to every age and generation. He compressed His message to us into writing. The ability to write and read are things we take for granted, but they are capacities given to those who are created in God's image. Humans are able to think, to communicate, to record in symbols, pass information between centuries, and make personal choices. Would God's message, His solution, not be worth pursuing? Genesis gives us the first clues. (By the way, humanity has an enemy complicit with death. He does not want people to realize they have a choice. He keeps us distracted, dancing to his tune.) Hearing God's voice requires re-tuned ears and purposeful discipline.

We need to get a feel for the whole story. A panoramic approach ties together the whole Bible consecutively. Those who lived before the Incarnation had a foretaste of God's promised solution, and we today can look back at the event that our BC/AD calendar is based upon. That Biblical progression from Genesis to Revelation (from before Time's beginning on into Eternity) records God's clues to us through many authors and over many centuries. Each writer records a new chapter of a single story—God and mankind's story. When we grasp a sense of the whole, we can much more fully appreciate the parts. If we "can't see the forest for the trees" in life, we can't know where we are, ourselves, or why.

⇓ **What's the heart of the story, the crux of it all?** In the opening verses of the Gospel of Luke, the author says he is giving "an account of the things that have been fulfilled among us...handed down...by eyewitnesses...so that you may know the certainty of the things you have been taught." The missionary to India, E. Stanley Jones, in *The Word Become Flesh* (in the devotion for Week 18—Sunday) calls those things that happened—that were fulfilled—the *Central Cosmic Fact*. "God appeared on a little planet to take us by the hand and put us back on the Way. This is news—Good News—comparatively speaking, the only Good News that ever reached our planet."

During the period of the appearance of the Messiah on earth after His resurrection, He gave two people an amazing encounter one evening. *Look up Luke 24:13-37, and try to "be there" overhearing.*

Who are the three people?

Who knows the most about the last three days?

What body of Scripture does the Stranger "open"?

Let's set the scene. It is the Sunday evening after the crucifixion of Jesus of Nazareth on Friday. His disciples are crushed and afraid. A dejected pair is walking home when a Stranger appears, and asks why they are so sad. (Imagine yourself to be one of them.) They reply, "Are you only a visitor to Jerusalem and do not know the things that have happened there in these days?" What irony! They pour out the story, and then the Stranger responds with these powerful words:

> How foolish you are, and how slow of heart to believe all that the prophets have spoken. Did not the Christ have to suffer these things and then enter his glory?" And beginning with Moses and all the Prophets, he explained to them what was said in all the Scriptures concerning himself.

They invite Him to eat with them, hanging on every word. When *Yeshua* breaks the bread, they recognize Him, perhaps by the nail scars in His hands. Suddenly the risen Christ disappears. Astounded, they run back to Jerusalem crying, "Were not our hearts burning within us while he talked with us on the road and opened the Scriptures to us?"

Would you like to have been there with your heart burning, too? Would you like to find out what the earliest believers heard and recorded for us, about what the Messiah explained that night?

Just think, we today have the same Old Testament Jesus was quoting from that night — i.e., "Moses and all the prophets." Wouldn't it be remiss not to trace what He said about His own identity from the Old Testament? (Even though we now have the New Testament, we'll know Him much better and appreciate what He fulfilled much more, if we give these well-placed earlier clues our attention.)

⇐ **Notice the ALL's** in the verses above, Luke 24:25-27: "*all* that was spoken, by Moses and *all* the prophets, in *all* the scriptures" — i.e. the Old Testament. That is all the written material the early believers had to work with in their proclamation of Jesus the Christ, the long promised "Anointed One," the "Messiah." *Consider what the resurrected Jesus said that night.* (Luke 24:25-27)

1. How familiar was the Stranger with Moses and the prophets, and who did He say they were talking about?

2. If you could grasp what He said "concerning himself," what difference might it make to you?

God's teaching methods are fascinating. Just imagine, how would <u>you</u> go about the problem of communicating from Eternity into Time? How would <u>you</u> start with humanity at the world's beginning and keep communicating throughout every generation? Examining the Bible, we find that our Creator used all kinds of vehicles to carry His truth — written accounts, ceremonies, holy places, festivals of celebration, and more. He laid a whole string of messianic clues given in "types" or previews, called "shadows," before the time of the Light's full arrival.

We may think of the Bible as focused on us and <u>our needs</u>. But for God, the focus is on our recognition of <u>His identity</u>. If only we would recognize Him, we would be drawn to Him. Look at these examples of how repeatedly and passionately God the Father and Jesus the Son disclosed their identity: *What are some things God reveals about Himself in these passages about <u>identity</u>?*

1. God revealing Himself to Moses: Exodus 3:1-6, 13-15.

2. Angels sent to Jesus' parents: Matthew 1:20-23, Luke 1:30-33.

3. God revealing the identity of the God-man:
   Matthew 3:15-17; 17:1-9.

4. Jesus identifying Himself on earth: John 6:46-51; 8:12
     and 58; 11:25-26; 14:6.

5. Jesus giving His disciples their "final exam": Mark 8:27-30,
     Luke 9:18-22

6. Jesus speaking from Heaven: Revelation 22:7, 13, 16

♥ **By now when we are living,** the Holy Spirit has revealed the Bible's whole story. We can examine the New Testament account of the Incarnation of the Son of God in the Gospels, as well as what the Holy Spirit soon revealed to the first believers, recorded in the Letters. We can check whether the new evidence corroborates the Old Testament. We've got the whole overview — so we hardly have an excuse for ignorance!

♥ *Are you willing to investigate God's testimony to the risen Christ?*

For Discussion:
What do you think about the Spirit's statement in I John 5:9-12?

Q. What two kinds of people does God say there are?

Q. What is the difference between them?

♥ *Which of the two do you believe yourself to be?*

Ω

About prayer: *God is the only one with the wisdom and authority to answer our deep questions and hungers. Asking Him to do so is our privilege, and His pleasure. Praying is a good place to start this quest. Talk with Him.*

Study 3

SEED

What is our human predicament?

(Beginning our quest where the Bible begins, Genesis)

Introduction: Have you ever played the game called "Clue"? It's a board game with the goal being to guess "who done it." Who committed the crime, in which location, and with what weapon? Everybody is fascinated with a murder mystery, the basis of countless books, plays, films and even games. We get more uncomfortable when murder reports flood our news media—about real murderers in our hometown.

Context: Where did murder start? Genesis records its appearance right in humanity's first family — one brother killing another. Death was unknown at the beginning of Creation. It was not God's plan.

What is man's seemingly unsolvable predicament? Have you ever known a human who didn't die, or isn't going to do so eventually? We never think of not dying. God's enemy wants us to imagine death was in the nature of things from the beginning, but it was not. We need to understand that something fundamental changed in Eden, something that has been passed on to the whole Adamic family, generation by generation: death. That catastrophic change is usually referred to as "the Fall." Our first parents "fell" away from their original state of fellowship with God.

Was God able to do anything to rescue humanity? Yes! God began immediately to take steps to solve this greatest of all problems. We have a record of what happened in the first three chapters of Genesis. Let's begin by examining the essence of this terrible rupture that began in the garden, was fought out in a garden, and was restored in a garden. (That's one panoramic summary: From Genesis, to the Passion, to the great Restoration.)

Using *ALL*'s "shadow-to-substance" study method, let's look at all three blocks of content: Old Testament history, the Incarnational events, and what the Spirit revealed thereafter in the New Testament.

⇐ **Looking backward at the history of mankind**, what clues can we get about the genesis of our problem from the book with that name?

Q. How did God evaluate His world at the creation? Genesis 1:31

Q. What did God tell Adam in Genesis 2:16-17?

Q. What was the enemy's goal behind his words in Genesis 3:4-5?

Q. What happened when Adam and Eve sided with Satan rather than God? Notice the results in Genesis 3:7-10.

Q. What did God promise about Eve's "seed"? Genesis 3:15

Q. How was their ban from Eden meant to help them? Genesis 3:22

⇓ **Let's skip forward to the arrival of the God-man,** recorded in the four Gospels. When the Messianic Seed — the seed of Mary – entered the world through the miracle of the Holy Spirit's visitation, a few Spirit-led people received Him as the long-promised Messiah. From the four Gospels, who was this person indicated to be?

➤ Matthew 1:18-25 – What was the miracle?

➤ Mark 1:1– What is Jesus' title?

> ➢ Luke 1:35 – What was the angel's message?

> ➢ John 1:1-5, 14 – Jesus is called *what*, and did *what*?

> ➢ John 1:29-34 – How did the Forerunner of the Messiah identify him?

What are samples of what He said about His own identity?

❖ John 14:6-11 – What is the astounding claim of verse 9?

❖ John 3:13-15 – What is the Son of Man's destiny?

❖ John 11:25-26 – " I AM the *what?"*

How did God prove His Son's identity? (See Acts 2:23-24, 32.)

⇒ **Moving forward from the visit of God to earth**, what do the New Testament letters reveal about Adam and Christ, the "First and Second Adam"?

1. From Romans 1:18-32, what is humanity's state, before God?

2. From Romans 2:1-16, and 3:10-12, who is righteous?

3. From Romans 3:21-31 and 5:17-19, how does anyone become "righteous" in God's sight?

4. How did death come into the world? (Match the Genesis story with Romans 5:12.)

5. In Romans 5:17-19, what did the First Adam's disobedience cause, and what two gifts do the obedience of the Second Adam win for us?

6. How did God reverse man's death sentence? I Corinthians 15:20-22 and 45-49 explain this amazing provision.

7. According to I Corinthians 15:42-52, what destiny comes to a person naturally from the First Adam? What destiny can be chosen through the Last Adam?

The Clue game reversed! Remember "Clue" – "*who* did it *where*, with what *instrument*?" It's about murder and death — things Adam's choice issued in. How can death be "undone"? Scripture reveals God's amazing answer to the seemingly inescapable death-sentence inherited by Adam's descendants. Human beings have all been "in Adam." We all come from his seed. We are in the line of Adam — the genealogical "head" of the human race. We came "into Adam" by birth. But God has provided a way to give life that overcomes death. God gifts the world with a Second Adam — a Second Man to head up the human race!

God provided an amazing means of escape. The Spirit of God must interpret to us this mystery that is so crucial to our condition. Those who claim the Second Adam's payment of their sin debt have, in God's sight, "died." We are freed from our captivity in Adam, by "death." We came into the First Adam by birth and we come into the Second Adam by birth, too, by rebirth. This transaction is explained in Scripture.

What amazing facts are explained in Romans 6:1-11?

Inevitably, we will all stay "in" Adam, unless, unless... some of us actually choose the Second Adam to be "in." What does I Corinthians 15:20-22 tell us about life and death?

Each of us needs to ask, *"Which Adam am I in?"*

Take a good look at the small word "in." Some say it is the most important relational word in the New Testament. From this look at man's original problem (the one we continue to face), be sure you understand the principle behind being "in Adam" or "in Christ." Every person is "in" one or the other. Our fallen state was not asked for. It was inherited. The other is chosen. Humans can't help being "in Adam" – the "head of our race." However, we can accept God's gift of a new Head, if we are willing to embrace His presence in us, and our being included "in Him."

Ephesians 1:7-10 reveals God's grace toward us. *What do you find there to be true of all who are IN Christ?*

The gift is "free," but it cost both the Father and the Son a terrible price to accomplish this deliverance. *Appropriating that gift personally can change your life, and settle your destiny.*

♥ *How do I respond to this amazing "in" disclosure?*

Prayer: *Dear Father, help me grasp your reversal of death. Help me make the choice to be __IN__ Christ, to access His life within now, and forever.*

Ω

Hold on to the SEED KEY to both Covenants!

For since death came through a man, the resurrection of the dead comes also through a man. For as in Adam all die, so in Christ all will be made alive.

I Corinthians 15:21-22

Study 4

SON

How was the Messianic Son to be identified?

(Based principally on Genesis)

Introduction: We have looked at the results of the Fall, at the promise of a "seed" who would someday reverse that disaster, and at how the Scriptures present Jesus as the 2nd Adam. The book of Genesis goes on to record humanity's continuing rebellion, God's judgment through the flood in Noah's time, the new start given to that family, and the folly of pride that brought another judgment — the confusion of languages. How was God going to restore a race gone so bad? How was He to tell them how much He loved them?

Try to imagine the difficulties of God-to-man communication. Remember that time is the only category humans live in, but God's dimension is eternal, time-less. The Scriptures speak of "before the beginning of time" or "before the world began." (Examples: II Timothy 1:9, John 17:5.) How could God get a message through to time-bound humanity? Well, how might you, a big human, speak to an ant? You'd have to become one to do it! That seems to be similar to what God decided to do.

⇓ **God chose to send a Second Adam into the world** right in the middle of history, at just the right time in God's sight. That amazing appearance we call "the Incarnation" — the presence of God on earth—"Emmanuel"—"God with us." E. Stanley Jones called it "God's redemptive invasion" (Week 17, Friday). Only God could have given us a new head of the race. The Second Adam defeated death, rose from the grave, and offers redemption to the whole world. A few years after the event, Paul explained it to Timothy in these terms:

> This grace was given us in Christ Jesus before the beginning of time, but it has now been revealed through the appearing of our Savior, Christ Jesus, who has destroyed death and has brought life and immortality to light through the gospel.
>
> II Timothy 1:9b-10

How difficult was that "appearing" to perceive? God in the form of a man was unknown. In fact, He might not be too welcome, appearing suddenly among a fallen people. He wasn't. Man killed God. It took the miracle of the resurrection of the promised Messiah to awaken even *Yeshua*'s disciples to His true identity. It took the outpoured gift from the Father and Son — the Holy Spirit — to awaken them to their Guide and Teacher. After all, He was the author of Scripture. (See II Timothy 3:16, II Peter 1:21.) The Holy Spirit began to unveil to the early Christians the preparatory "shadows" and clues God had given throughout the Old Testament times, to help them corroborate the evidence. (See examples of the term "shadows" in Colossians 2:17, Hebrews 8:5, and 10:1.) We today have the advantage of the completed Scriptures to turn to. How amazing it must have seemed to those in the first century AD, as the connections were coming together for them for the first time!

⇐ **What if we had been at Emmaus that evening after the Resurrection,** hearing *Yeshua* explain how the Scriptures spoke of Him? (See Luke 24.) We would surely have heard Him point to the foundation God laid when He chose out one man, Abraham, with one son, Isaac. From this "line of the promise" would come the family from which the Messiah would eventually be born. This was one clue that had to match at the time of His arrival. The Savior of the world would have to be a son of Abraham. Abraham was head of a branch of humanity called "the Hebrews," or "Israelites," from "Israel" — the new name Abraham's grandson Jacob was given. (Genesis 32:28)

God's interactions with the Hebrews are at the heart of the Old Testament, and are the backdrop of the New. We need to understand God's covenant relationship with His chosen people — the patriarchal community through which He would be blessing the whole world, eventually, through Abraham's offspring, the Messiah.

Q. *What are some of the steps in the progression of God's covenant with Abraham that appear in Genesis?*

Genesis 12:1-3

Genesis 15:1-6

Genesis 17:1-14

Genesis 22:18

"Seed," not "seeds: Notice that Paul, a Hebrew scholar, points out that the promise to Abraham was to come through his "seed" — singular. (See Galatians 3:16-19.)

A fast forward: David's Psalm of thanksgiving years later, Psalm 105, gives us quick overview of early Israelite history. It starts with God's covenant with Abraham, Isaac, and Jacob (recorded in Genesis) and continues with the Hebrews' preservation in Egypt through Joseph, goes on to the building of a nation in Moses' time some 400 years later (recorded in Exodus), and on to becoming heirs of the Promised Land in Joshua's time.

As we go back to the covenant people's foundation, we find that Abraham and Isaac's Mt. Moriah experience is one of Scripture's great "shadow" previews — sometimes called "types." Abraham's great test in Genesis 22:1-19 occurred 2,000 years before Christ, on a certain "Mt. Moriah," before there even was a "Jerusalem." *Yeshua* was sacrificed on Mt. Moriah 2000 years later! How perfectly God placed His Son's sacrifice. How carefully He prefigured it! Consider how graphic a preview was enacted through Abraham and Isaac — in the light of the later sacrifice of the Son on that same Mt. Moriah. This Son actually did rise from the dead — physically not figuratively! The Mt. Moriah experience is an indelible picture of the Messiah as the Father's Son.

Try to imagine how you might have felt if you were Abraham, or if you were Isaac, in order to get a glimpse of the cost to the Father and Son at the Savior's cross. The shadow in this early time was thrown backward from a reality that would eventually happen. We need to remember that the realities themselves are eternal in God's sight. After Christ's passion and enthronement, the Holy Spirit interpreted this shadowy event. *What clue does Hebrews 11:17-19 give as to what Abraham may have expected?*

⇓ **While Jesus was on earth, exactly what claims did He make?** What are some of the things He said about Abraham? *Imagine yourself to be a local person listening, one who took deep pride in being a "child of Abraham," the father of their nation. How might you have responded to Jesus during this encounter in John 8:31-42, and 52-58?*

What was Jesus saying about Himself, and about Abraham?

What did He mean claiming, "before Abraham was, I AM"? If that were true, who was—is—Jesus?

Look at the parable Jesus told about "Father Abraham." What was He predicting about His own resurrection in Luke 16:19-31?

⇒ **When the early disciples were spreading the Good News**, what was it in Abraham's life that they appealed to? This was the legacy of Abraham's attitude toward God that holds up throughout all generations. It is called "reckoned righteousness." (Reckoned means "credited" or "imputed" — gifted.) This is the only kind of righteousness God accepts. Paul explains the difference between "work-earned" and "reckoned" righteousness. *According to this explanation in Romans 4:1-12 and 22-25, how can anyone become "justified"?*

Faith is the subject of Hebrews 11, in which Abraham is memorialized in verses 8-19. Notice the amplifying wording of two translations of Hebrews 11:1 (good to memorize):

> "Faith is the substance of things hoped for,
>   the evidence of things not seen." (KJV)

> "Now faith is being sure of what we hope for
>   and certain of what we do not see." (NIV)

What qualifies anyone to become a "daughter or son of Abraham" and therefore to expect the future privileges that go with that relationship? *Consult three places where this is explained:*

Romans 4:11

Romans 9:6-8

Galatians 3:26-29

What kind of righteousness does God tell us to count on? We are encouraged by Scripture to rely on a marvelous exchange.

According to II Corinthians 5:21, who gets what? And why?

Who is a "daughter or son of Abraham"? Jesus knew the end from the beginning. He knew what was coming in the future. He spoke of a future time when some will "sit down at the table with Abraham, Isaac, and Jacob." (That is previewed in Matthew 8:11.)

♥ *Do I expect to be there?*

On what basis?

Prayer: *Dear Father, Thank You for the Messianic Son, Yeshua, the Lord Jesus. Thank You for His sacrifice on Mt. Moriah to take my sin payment and gift me with His righteousness. I am amazed by the gracious transfer assured to me. Awaken me to its meaning, and to the One who paid the price for this exchange. I pray in the crucified Son's name.*

Ω

Hold on to the SON KEY to both Covenants!

By faith Abraham, when God tested him, offered Isaac as a sacrifice. He who had received the promises was about to sacrifice his one and only son, even though God had said to him, "It is through Isaac that your offspring will be reckoned." Abraham reasoned that God could raise the dead, and figuratively speaking, he did receive Isaac back from death.

Hebrews 11:17-19

Study 5

LAMB

How did God accomplish Israel's redemption? How is this like our own?

(Drawn principally from the book of Exodus)

Introduction: The most repeated story of the Old Testament is the Exodus. The book by that name records the Hebrews' deliverance out of slavery in Egypt, when God rescued the family of Abraham, Isaac, and Jacob. *Trace the Hebrew saga in Canaan and Egypt that spanned over 600 years:*

About 2000 BC - The original promise to Abraham: Genesis 15:13-16

About 1800 BC - Joseph's trust in God's promise to his forefathers: Genesis 50:24-26

About 1400 BC - Fulfillment under Moses: Exodus 12:40-42; 13:19

(Notice Joshua 24:32.)

Context: The Exodus deliverance occurred after the Israelites' 400 years of captivity in Egypt. God chose Moses to deliver them, assisted by his brother Aaron. A great struggle ensued between Pharaoh and God, mediated by Moses. Pharaoh was unwilling to let his slave community go, even at God's command. After nine acts of warning, all resisted by proud Pharaoh, the tenth plague finally brought deliverance from captivity into freedom. The final judgment on arrogance and unbelief was the death of Egypt's first-born sons.

What importance does this deliverance hold for those of us living over 3,000 years later? If you search through the Old Testament, you will find that the Exodus event — deliverance through the blood of sacrificial lambs — is God's *basic redemptive act* for Israel. As we compare the events involved in Christ's death, we discover that God's *redemptive analogy through the Passover lamb* was being fulfilled by the final Lamb. This connection was revealed by the Spirit, after it was accomplished. Notice the progression of this panoramic process, symbolized as: $\Leftarrow \Downarrow \Rightarrow$

$\Leftarrow$ **How did the Hebrew community escape the judgment of death** poured out on Pharaoh's people? The story is recorded in Exodus, chapters 11 to 14. *In Exodus 12, examine what happened that night:*

Exodus 12:1-3, 6, and 14-20:
When did God tell His people to start their new calendar?

Exodus 12:5-7:
What part did a lamb play in this drama?

Exodus 12:7, 13:
What was the function of blood?

By whom was the blood to be seen?

Exodus 12:24-27:
What is the meaning of the term "Passover"?

Exodus 12:29-30:
What was revealed to be the result of God's judgment?

⇔ **Although the original Exodus Passover happened long ago, it is still rehearsed yearly** by the Jewish community everywhere. God commanded them to do it perpetually, as recorded in Exodus 12:42. A few months after their escape to Sinai, God instituted seven yearly "feasts unto the Lord," beginning with Passover.

Centuries later, the Messiah's New Covenant community used Old Testament language when they spoke of Jesus' fulfillment of the Passover. Today's Messianic Jews (who do believe that *Yeshua* was and is the Messiah) also celebrate these feasts. Gentile believers can learn much from them, too.

⇓ **At the time of the Incarnation, how did the Forerunner, John the Baptist, introduce Jesus?** Notice the culturally understood term John used for the Messiah when he pointed out *Yeshua* in John 1:29 and 36. As a devout Jew, John well knew the role of the lamb that was sacrificed each day at the Temple, and especially the Passover Lamb.

Yeshua **told His disciples that He had come to die** – "to give His life as a ransom." Matthew 20:28 and Mark 10:45 record His statement. Like the lamb's blood that protected the Hebrews from the death angel the night of the Exodus, the blood of the Lamb of God is the ransom that protects from spiritual death as well.

The prophet Isaiah was given a preview of the Messiah's death. *Read Isaiah 53 carefully to answer:*

In what significant details does Isaiah foresee the mystery of the Savior's passion and death?

What was the Apostle John's understanding of Isaiah 53, as recorded in John 12:37-41?

Just before the Messiah became the final Passover lamb, He gave new meaning to the Passover Feast. The night before *Yeshua*'s sacrifice, He served the Passover Supper in light of the true Lamb's blood. This "cup of the new covenant" is recorded by Matthew, Mark, and Luke. John fills out much more of what Jesus said that night. When Christians celebrate the Lord's Supper, they usually read these verses from the Gospels, or the words of I Corinthians 11. *Look again at them in light of their deep Old Testament roots:*

Passover's new meaning: Matthew 26:27-28; Luke 22:20

The early church's Lord's Supper: I Corinthians 11:24-25

⇒ **After Christ rose from the grave, the disciples broke forth** with the wonderful Good News of *the Second Adam*'s having conquered death! They begged people to put their faith in God's *Son*, vindicated by His resurrection. They explained that cleansing and redemption were available to Israel through the final Passover *Lamb*'s blood. *Think through some of the New Testament passages in terms of the Lamb's blood:*

➤ Romans 3:23-26

➤ Colossians 1:14, 20

➤ Ephesians 1:7

➤ I John 1:7

➤ Acts 20:28

↓ **The book of Revelation requires a new teaching symbol** for the final references to Jesus as the Lamb of God, revealed from Heaven.

NOTE: *A narrow pointer (↓) indicates Christ's later appearance when He gave a last message from heaven – rather than the thicker Incarnational symbol (⇓) for His thirty-three-year lifespan on earth.*

↓ **A final message from Jesus, the Lamb of God:** The Book of Revelation was given from <u>God</u> to <u>Jesus</u> to deliver through an <u>angel</u> to <u>John</u>. (Revelation 1:1-2, and 22:16.) John was the only disciple of the original twelve still alive. The ten had been killed for their unwavering testimony to the resurrection of Jesus. *See the Lamb as the center of worship in the Revelation:*

Revelation 5:6, 12

Revelation 7:9, 14

Revelation 14:3-4

Revelation's culmination — the Lamb's wedding and rule:

The Lamb's marriage: Revelation 19:9 and 21:9

The Lamb on the Throne: Revelation 22:1-4

The Lamb tells us even more about Himself through the names He calls Himself at the close of Revelation. They point both backward and forward.

Circle the 11 Messianic names He used:

> I am the Alpha and the Omega, the First and the Last, the Beginning and the End. . . . I, Jesus, have sent my angel to give you this testimony for the churches. I am the Root and the Offspring of David, and the bright Morning Star. Revelation 22:13, 16

As Alpha and Omega, Jesus is <u>all</u>. Like bookends to the Bible, Genesis begins and Revelation ends in a garden. The *seed* of Eve, the *Second Adam*, has crushed the head of the serpent. The *Son* has come in the flesh and "tabernacled with us." The *Host* has redefined the Passover. The *Lamb* of God has been sacrificed on Mt. Moriah, and has become the Lion of Judah. The saga of Redemption is completed. The ultimate *Prophet's* Revelation previews the eventual banquet of the *Bridegroom*, the Messianic *King* of David's line, in all His glory. The "morning star" announces a new day. Lo, the end is ending, and the Beginning is beginning!

⇔ **What can the Spirit of God help us gather from this panorama?** It stretches from the death of the first lamb (evident in the skins God gave as a covering) at the time of the Fall in Eden to the appearance of "the Lamb that was slain" at the end of Revelation. This mystery was progressively revealed through many authors over many centuries. They all tie to one historic fact, the sacrifice of the Lamb of God. God had been building one principle and revelation upon another. Some facts that we would do well to recognize and value are these:

a. **The seriousness of sin before a holy God**. Sin brings forth death. The life of an individual is in the blood. "Without the shedding of blood is no remission of sin." (Leviticus 17:11)

b. **The Passover is God's supreme object lesson** demonstrating *substitutional* atonement — one life substituted for another.

In early times, God mercifully provided for atonement through the life of an animal in place of the death of a man or woman. Ever since the final Lamb gave His life as an atonement for the sins of the world, no animal sacrifices are needed. Hebrews 9:11-14 compares the worth of the Son's blood with an animal's blood. *To Whom is the Lamb's blood presented, and by Whom is the blood most valued?*

In God's sight, "worthy is the Lamb who was slain" to receive worship! He is pleased by our worship of the One who died for us, that we might live forever! We are freed from bondage to sin to live new lives, indwelt by the holiness of the sinless Lamb. Amazing love, amazing result!

♥ *How might I better value the blood of Jesus as God would have me?*

Prayer: *Lord, I am helpless to save myself from my sin problem. I thank You, Father, for providing a way. I worship You, Jesus—Lamb of God. You sheltered me from sin's death penalty, for your blood was substituted for mine. Spirit of God, awaken me to the value my Heavenly Father places on the Son's blood! Deepen my understanding, Lord, and my love for the Lamb who gave His life for me!*

Ω

Hold on to the LAMB KEY to both Covenants!

The next day John saw Jesus coming toward him and said, "Look, the Lamb of God, who takes away the sin of the world!"

John 1:29

Study 6

TWO

How are the two Testaments integrated?

(Parenthetic reference material between ALL's seven Messiah portraits)

Introduction: Basic to the whole Bible is the experience of "covenant" between God and man. The "first covenant" usually refers to God's relationship with Abraham and his descendants, the people of Israel. Jeremiah 31:31, 33 predicts a "new covenant" to come. It widens to include all believers in God's Messiah, whether Jew or Gentile. In the New Testament, the whole book of Hebrews compares, contrasts, and explains the two covenants' relationship.

⇔**The Old and New Covenants are like the two floors of one home.**

Not understanding the relationship between the two covenants has caused a huge relational problem over the centuries! The Biblical attitude toward the two is deeply respectful, intertwined, and successive. The two could be pictured as the first and second floor of the same home. The lower story is the foundation from which the upper story rises. Either one is incomplete without the other. If the foundation is missing, the upper structure has no firm base. If the upper structure is missing, the crowning expansion is missing. Either one alone stands exposed "without a roof." The roof is God's eternal purpose displayed in its full glory. Ephesians 2:19-22 explains the reality of God's spiritual temple today, calling the Messiah "the chief cornerstone."

Scripture moves from the First Covenant base line to the New Covenant reality. Biblical comparisons and contrasts are therefore made possible. We are assured that the process was always in God's eternal plan as He was progressively working out His redemptive purposes. (See Ephesians 1:3-10.)

Both covenants are critical for the believer to appreciate, understand, and enter into. Christians cannot fully experience God's message without becoming bi-cultural — knowing their own, and the Hebrew culture. Becoming conversant in the history, language, and culture of the Hebrew people equips us to grasp the Scriptures in a far deeper way.

When we say the Messiah _fulfilled_ the Old Testament, we must not think that means we should dispense with the past. To deeply understand what the Messiah fulfilled, we must know from the Old Testament who He was foreshadowed to be and what He was predicted to do. Our New Testament understanding must be _filled full_ by the Old. In the Scriptures, God provided for our unending search into the mysteries and glories of the Messiah, giving us layer after layer of clues, pictures, weavings, symbols, and "types."

Jesus/*Yeshua* Himself was thoroughly Jewish in His linage, upbringing, and daily life. He taught in the synagogue, revered the Old Testament, and quoted it regularly. He communicated in Jewish terms and primarily with Jewish people.

ALL **focuses on seven portraits or roles of this marvelous Messiah whom we are seeking to know and love in fullness.** These roles are all based in the Old Testament. We might call the Old Testament God's "picture book." Its script constitutes the ABC's of spiritual vocabulary. The next pages give a basic outline of the Covenant with Israel in Moses' time. Each aspect listed is profound — inexhaustible to study in a lifetime!

When God built the Hebrews into a nation, He gave them basic building blocks of a Godly society. The Old Covenant includes:

    I.   What? The Law – their life principles

    II.   When? The Feasts – their calendar

    III.   Who? The Priesthood – their leadership

    IV.   Where? The Tabernacle – their worship

We might be moved to add a question V. "Why?" The Fall necessitated protections between humans, and so laws and ordinances were entrusted to the priesthood to guide the community. Secondly, God wanted them to know His character, and become godly. He longed for all to be well with them. We can hear His longing in Deuteronomy 5:29. Finally, He was preparing the way for the arrival of the Seed, the world's Redeemer.

Short summaries of Hebrew history can be found in Psalm 105 and Acts 7:1-47, Stephen's sermon to Israel, for which he was martyred.

NOTE: The following pages give thumbnail information about the Law, Tabernacle, Priesthood, and Feasts at the time of Moses' ministry as mediator of the Old Covenant at Mt. Sinai. Study 6 provides a background to Studies 7 and 8, which focus on how the Messiah fulfilled the Old Covenant and initiated the New, as PRIEST and HOST. Studies 7 and 8 amplify the relationship between the two covenants and explain more about the function of the Law.)

I. *THE LAW*

Where is the Law found in Scripture? This body of instruction is recorded in the books of Moses, called the *Torah* in Hebrew. The Ark of the Covenant in the Tabernacle (containing the Ten Commandments) is at the heart of Israel's national life. The Law's origin and the Hebrews' interaction with it, is chronicled in Exodus, Leviticus, Numbers, and Deuteronomy.

> Exodus 20-40 records the moral and ceremonial Law that God gave to Moses on Mt. Sinai, including instructions for the Tabernacle, Priesthood, and Feasts.
> Leviticus: the Levitical priesthood's offerings, ordination, and laws.
> Numbers: Israel's arrangements and wilderness wanderings.
> Deuteronomy: second rehearsal of Israel's history, warnings, blessings.

> OLD: The Law appears throughout, as Israel interacts with it.
> NEW: The Law states God's standard, reveals our sin, and is our baseline to appreciate *God's grace,* operative throughout history.

What are the ten principles God has given (Exodus 20:1-17 and Deuteronomy 5:1-21) to help humanity in relating to Him and to each other? *Number them and write a key word or phrase for each:*

What does the New Testament reveal about the relationship between the two covenants? *In these passages, which comparisons are made – in terms of "promise," or "glory," or "a legal will," or "righteousness"?*

Romans 3:19-31

Galatians 3:6

II Corinthians 3:17-4:6

Hebrews 9:11-22

II. THE TABERNACLE

Then have them make a sanctuary for me, and I will
dwell among them. Make this tabernacle and all its
furnishings exactly like the pattern I will show you.

Exodus 25:8-9

The Tabernacle "pattern "— articles, dimensions, construction,
materials: Exodus 25-27 and 35-38.

THE TABERNACLE VIEWED FROM THE OUTSIDE:

A. Linen fence around enclosure – (100x50 cubits): Exodus 27:9-19
B. Curtained entrances to courtyard and the Holy Place
C. Priests, Levites, animals, and people participating in sacrifices
D. Tabernacle (15x45 feet or 10x30 cubits) with four layers of coverings
E. The *Shekina* glory cloud rising from above the Mercy Seat

Two articles visible in the courtyard outside: Exodus 27:9-19

       1. The Brazen Altar *for burnt sacrifices:* Exodus 27:1-8*
       2. The Laver *for washing:* Exodus 38:8

* Offerings were to be made at only one place: Deuteronomy 12:1-14.

INSIDE THE TABERNACLE:

(Structure made of acacia wood planks covered with gold, held up
with rings and bars; curtains in front of the Holy Place and Most Holy
Place.)

The Holy Place – seen only by priests and Levites, daily

       3. The Golden seven-flame Lampstand, *for light:* Ex. 25:31-40
       4. The Bread of the Presence, *for representation:* Ex. 25:23-30
       5. The Golden Incense Altar, *for intercession:* Ex. 37:25-29

The Most Holy Place – seen only by the High Priest, yearly

       6. The Ark of the Covenant, *holding the Law:* Ex.25:10-16
       7. The Mercy Seat, *the throne of grace:* Ex. 25:17-22

*On the accompanying drawings, pencil in letters and numbers at
their specified locations for these aspects:*

      A-E: the visible aspects from outside (listed above)

      1-7: the articles (listed above) used in Tabernacle worship

What happened at the first erection of the Tabernacle at Mt. Sinai?
(Exodus 40:34-35)

TABERNACLE (without its four coverings)

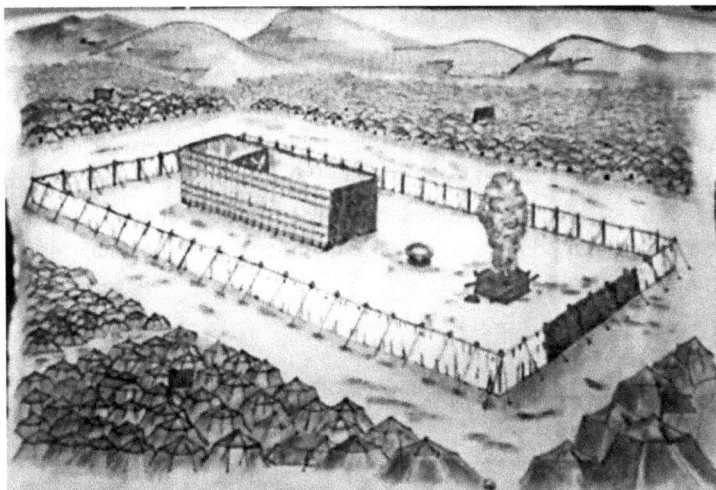

CEF flannel graph photo KB

SURROUNDING TRIBAL CAMPS: EAST: Moses, Aaron, and Levites, plus Zebulun, Judah, Issachar SOUTH: Simeon, Reuben, Gad WEST: Benjamin, Ephraim, Manasseh: NORTH: Asher, Dan, Naphtali

TABERNACLE DRAWING: (top is north)

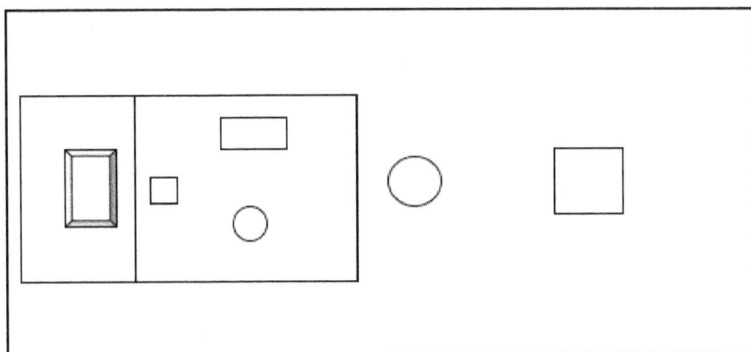

(Study 7 amplifies the Messiah's fulfillment of the Tabernacle's symbolism and purpose.)

III. THE FEASTS

Where are God's "Feasts unto the Lord" commanded? The Feasts are the subject of Exodus 12 (Passover's basic text), Exodus 23:14-17; Leviticus 16, 23, 25; Numbers 28, 29, and Deuteronomy 16, and more.

When were they celebrated? The seven feasts were celebrated within the three seasons specified in Exodus 23:14. (*Seven* seems to be God's clue word for "complete.") In contrast to our solar calendar, God's calendar is lunar (timed with the moon – festivals usually at full moon – helpful with no electricity!)

WEEKLY FEAST: the Sabbath.

ANNUAL FEASTS circle the seasons by the agricultural rhythms.

Spring Feasts:

    1. *Pesach* – Passover – 14th day of Ist month

    2. Unleavened Bread – I week concurrent with Passover

    3. First Fruits – the first Sunday after Passover

Summer begins: Feast 50 days after First Fruits:

    4. *Shavuot* - Feast of Weeks (7 x 7 + 1= 50) or Pentecost

Fall Feasts:

    5. *Rosh Hashanah* – Trumpets – Ist day of 7th month

    6. *Yom Kippur* – Day of Atonement – 10th day of 7th month (a fast)

    7. *Sukkot* – Ingathering, or Tabernacles, or Booths – 15th day of 7th month for a week, followed by an "8th day" (new beginning) feast

WHOLE YEAR FEASTS:

    1. The *Shmitah* – the Sabbatical year – every 7th year – the land is to rest and all consumer debts are to be canceled.

    2. The *Yovel* – the JUBILEE year – every 50th year – the land is to rest, all land is to be returned to the original owners, and the mortgages are canceled.

7th year LAND REST, and 7 x 7 + 1= 50 JUBILEE YEAR: Leviticus 25

A. Visualizing the Feasts according to the _agricultural_ cycle

(Exodus.23:14-17; Leviticus 23:5, 15-16, 33)

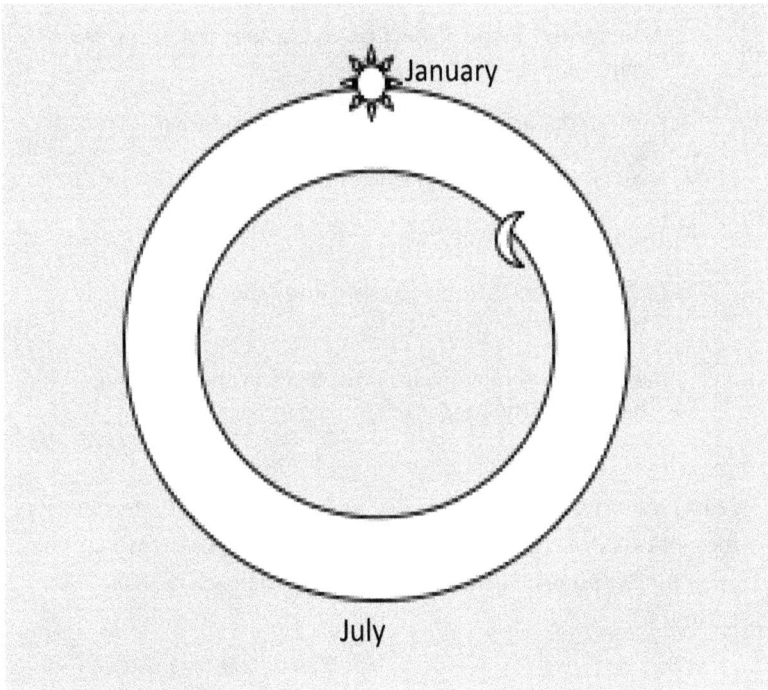

Write it in: _On the outer circle above, mark "Jan., Feb.," etc. for the solar month, clockwise. On the inner circle, place a symbol for each annual feast on its approximate Hebrew lunar month._ Passover starts on the 14th of the Hebrew lunar first month (solar March/April), Tabernacles on the 15th of the seventh month (solar Sept. /Oct.).

B. Visualizing the Feasts by the yearly "remembering"

1. Passover — saved from death, delivered, freed from bondage

2. Unleavened Bread — hurried to escape and cross sea miraculously

3. First Fruits — arose out of Red Sea, delivered alive

4. Feast of Weeks — Law given at Mt. Sinai

5. Trumpets — warning time

6. Day of Atonement — blood taken into Tabernacle's Holy of Holies yearly

7. Tabernacles — remembered dwellings in the wilderness, harvests in the Land

Feasts were "teaching platforms." (See Exodus 23:15.) Understanding these dates and happenings at deeply cultural occasions can help open the Scriptures. Related to which Feast did each of these events occur?

_____ The feast celebrated after the nation's circumcision at Gilgal. Joshua 5:8-12

_____ King Solomon's celebration at the First Temple's dedication: I Kings 8:1-2, 65-66 (Clue: Leviticus 23:34-36)

_____ Ezra reads the Law to the Israelites after the captivity: Nehemiah 8:1-12, 14, 18 (Clue: Deuteronomy 31:11)

C. Visualizing the Feasts historically (an _eschatological_ view)

✝

ETERNITY (former days) 1 2 3 | 4 (latter days) 5 6 7 ETERNITY

————————————————————————▶

TIME

Spring Feasts: completed during Incarnation and 50 days later:

1 Passover: Jesus' sacrificial death

2. Unleavened Bread: His burial

3. First Fruits: His resurrection

4. Pentecost: Holy Spirit poured out on believers

(Summer: sowing & reaping – "the Times of the Gentiles")

Fall Feasts: uncompleted, promised, and expected:

5. Trumpets: Jesus' promised return

6. Day of Atonement: Israel sees "whom they have pierced"

7. Tabernacles: the final Ingathering of all believers

Cross lines on this chart, matching summer & each unfinished feast on the left with Scriptures on the right:

(Summer)	Zechariah 12:10, Revelation 1:7
5. Trumpets	I Thess. 4:16-17, I Cor. 15:51-52
6. Day of Atonement	Romans 11:25, Matthew. 24:14
7. Tabernacles	Zechariah 14:16-17, Rev. 21:3

IV. THE PRIESTHOOD

Where is the Priesthood found in operation in Scripture?

- It is instituted in Exodus, and given instructions in detail in Leviticus.
- It is the operative leadership in Numbers and Deuteronomy.
- It continues from Tabernacle times into Temple times.
- It interacts with the nation and prophets throughout the Old Testament and is officiating at the Temple at the time of Christ.

Many priest passages seem obscure in the books of Moses, describing the priesthood's garments and duties as they led the community to follow the moral and ceremonial law. With study, however, their typology is rich in details that make our Lord Jesus' person and work all the more precious. Special areas of study include their garments in Exodus 28 and 39, consecration in Exodus 29, offerings in Leviticus 6 and 7, ordination in Leviticus 8, rules in Leviticus 21, 22, clans in Numbers 3 and 4, and duties in Numbers 18, 19.

What did the Temple's destruction (70 AD) do to the priesthood?
It ended it. The whole sacrificial system collapsed with no Temple. Jesus prophesied that this would happen. (See Matthew 24:1- 2.)

Why is the Levitical priesthood laid aside now? With the sacrifice of the last and perfect Lamb, the need for further sacrifices ended, as Hebrews 10:9 explains. *(Lesson 7 amplifies the role of the Messiah as our Great High Priest.)*

Ω

Resources for study of the Law, Priesthood, Tabernacle, Temple, and Feasts:

The Life and Times of Jesus the Messiah by Alfred Edersheim sets the Jewish biblical scene at the Messiah's arrival. This classic was first published in Oxford in 1886 and has been reprinted repeatedly.

The Tabernacle by Henry William Soltau (Kregel Publications, reprinted 1971).

Genesis to Deuteronomy by C.H. Mackintosh (Loizeaux Brothers, 1972).

Christ in the Passover by Rosen is one of many texts by Messianic Jewish believers, integrating the O. T. Feasts with N. T. teaching.

Celebrate the Feasts by Zimmerman helps Christians learn "how to."

Rose Publishing charts on the Tabernacle, Temple, Priesthood, etc.

(See the Bibliography for more information.)

NOTE: This Lesson 6, TWO, about the two covenants, has been parenthetical between ALL's portraits of the Messiah. Its purpose is to inform the study of this formative period in the history of God's people, when the Law, Tabernacle, Priesthood, and Feasts were instituted. We resume now with the next portrait of the Messiah, as PRIEST.

Study 7

PRIEST

How can human beings be brought into fellowship with a holy God?

(Drawn mainly from Exodus, Leviticus, John, and Hebrews)

Introduction: Considering the huge gap between a holy God and sinful mankind, how can they be reconciled and have fellowship? God undertook to provide a way. Mediation was necessary. God assigned certain representatives of the community to take the role of priests. Priests represented the people before God. Prophets (the subject of another chapter) in contrast, represented God to man. The priestly role progressed from the Levitical priesthood in Old Testament times, to Christ's fulfillment as our Great High Priest, to our present reality. Now all members of the believing community are called "the priesthood of believers." (I Peter 2:5) What an amazing privilege!

Context: After the Fall, God longed to bring man back into fellowship with Himself, and He put a progressive plan into action. He chose to reveal Himself to one man and his family, so that eventually they could communicate the plan to unbelieving humanity. *ALL*'s Study 4 focused on the account of Abraham's call to become the forefather of the *Son* who would bless all nations. The family of Abraham, Isaac, and Jacob moved to Egypt to avoid famine, became captives there 400 years, and grew possibly to two million. On schedule (see God's promise in Genesis 15:13), God took them to a new stage in His plan: nationhood. *ALL*'s Study 5 focused on the *Lamb,* the key player in the story of the Hebrews' escape out of slavery to the Sinai desert. In an isolated place with little food or water, God provided for them miraculously and began to mold this motley multitude into a community organized according to His careful instructions.

⇐ **It's a fascinating story!** Exodus chapters 16-40 specify the Hebrews' vital necessities. Who would lead them, how would they survive, what principles would order their society, where would their rallying point be, when would they do what, and where would they eventually settle? *(Study 6 gave a thumbnail sketch of major aspects of the First Covenant on which the Second is based, including a sketch of the Tabernacle.)*

Chapter by chapter, God's pattern for their life is laid out. These commands revealed the character of God, after whom they were to pattern their lives. The laws and ordinances that God gave were designed to bring blessing and harmony to the community. They also provided for protection from each other in a fallen world.

Having seen God's judgment on Egypt, the Israelites feared God. "You talk to Him, Moses," they said. Smoking Mt. Sinai frightened them. Their memories were so short that when Moses went up the mountain to receive God's law and was gone 40 days, they asked Aaron for a golden calf idol and lusted to go back to Egypt, the land of their bondage. (Not too different from some of us?) Moses pled with God to spare them. God revealed to Moses the shocking fact that He actually loved these faithless people so much that He was willing to come to live in the heart of their camp to have fellowship with them. How on earth could they survive the power and holiness of God? He spelled out the way.

God told them where and when and how they could come to Him safely. At the heart of the camp, Moses was to build a "Tabernacle":

> Then have them make a sanctuary for me, and I will dwell among them. Make this tabernacle and all its furnishings exactly like the pattern I will show you.
>
> Exodus 25:8-9

A thumbnail summary of the Sinai Covenant:

1. <u>What</u>? Ten commands are to guide your relationship with your God and with each other. (See Ex. 20:1-17.)

2. <u>Where</u>? I will come to live in the center of your camp, in a tent like yours. My "Tabernacle" will have an outer court, the Holy Place, and the Most Holy Place in which to place the Ark of the Covenant and its cover. I will meet with you at the Mercy Seat. (See Ex 25:22.)

3. <u>How</u>? Set up the seven articles I describe, representing the steps that lead to fellowship with Me. (See Ex. 25-30.)

4. <u>When</u>? Daily, weekly, monthly and yearly, my calendar will center your lives around me in regular rhythms. These times of gathering will afford occasions for remembering my Law, teaching the generations, and celebrating together. (See Leviticus 23 and 25.)

5. <u>Who</u>? Since I am One, and you are thousands, a representative way to come into my Presence must be provided. In the Holy Place, Levitical priests will place twelve loaves before me to represent your tribes in our fellowship together. Your High Priest will symbolically "carry you" into my presence on his shoulders (the ephod) with your names engraved on two onyx stones, and by the twelve gemstones on his breastplate. (See Exodus 28:6-14 and Exodus 39:2-14).

In the books of Exodus, Leviticus, Numbers, and Deuteronomy these principles are spelled out. The history of the Israelites' repeated progress and remissions and restorations are chronicled. God instructs them to pass on the Covenant and its practices obediently from generation to generation, for their own blessing. They were to be taught three times a year at His "feasts unto the Lord." *Notice how perpetual the rehearsals of these ordinances were to be, and what purpose they were to fulfill:*

Exodus 12:14, 24-28

Leviticus 23:1, 14, 41

Since the Tabernacle is the major subject of about **fifty** chapters of the Bible, it seems obvious that God means us to learn much through this teaching tool. These principles were repeated for 1400 years in Tabernacle and Temple worship. Every day the sacrifices acted out God's provision for remission of sin through substitution. They were saying, in effect, "The lamb's blood is allowed to substitute for your own death penalty. You may come to be cleansed from sin so that you may have fellowship with Me."

(The Tabernacle can be a huge study in itself. It is briefly summarized in Study 6, pages 54 and 55.)

Tabernacle ceremonies taught the basic principles of sinful mankind's approach to a holy God. What was the purpose for each of the seven articles found in the three areas of the Tabernacle?

Write in their purpose (shown on page 54) on the graph below:

SEVEN ARTICLES OF THE TABERNACLE (Exodus 25-30)

OUTER COURT:
1.Brazen Altar_____   2.Laver _____

HOLY PLACE:
      3.Lampstand_____   4.Loaves_____   5.Incense
Altar_____

MOST HOLY PLACE:
6.Ark of the Covenant _____   7.Mercy Seat_____

If you were a Levitical priest, when it was your week of service, you would administer the sacrifices in the outer court, and the Holy Place. You could not enter the Most Holy Place.

If you were High Priest, just once a year you would take the blood of atonement into the Holy of Holies. (See Hebrews 9.) God promised that He would meet with His people "between the cherubim above the Mercy Seat" in the Most Holy Place. (See Exodus 25:21-22.) The atoning blood was placed on the atonement cover — the Mercy Seat — once a year, above the Ten Commandments in the Ark below, symbolically "covering" the broken law.

If you were among the rest of the Hebrew camp, you could see the *Shekina* (literally "residence") glory cloud of the Lord rising from between the cherubim on the Mercy seat, manifested in a cloud by day and pillar of fire by night. (Exodus 40:34-38) These details are deeply meaningful as we apply them to the priesthood to which believers are called in the New Covenant. (I Peter 2:5, 9)

⇓ **Moving now to the God-man's visit to earth,** let us see how He spoke of Himself in regard to Tabernacle symbolism. Notice that *Yeshua* prefaced many of His statements with "I AM." *See Exodus 3:13-15 for the significance of the "I AM" connection.*

Look at some of the aspects of the Tabernacle that Jesus said "I am" about, or demonstrated by His words or life:

♦ The Door - John 10:7

♦ The Sacrifice – John 10:11, 17-18

♦ The Sanctifier – John 13:8-12

♦ The Light – John 8:12

♦ The Bread – John 6:35

♦ The Intercessor – John 17:20-21 (See Hebrews 7:25.)

♦ The Law-keeper – John 8:29

♦ The Mercy Seat – John 14:9

Jesus the High Priest, intercessor at the Altar of Incense, carried His own blood into God's Presence, into the true Holy of Holies. *See how these Scriptures depict Him:*

1. For whom is the Great High Priest interceding on the eve of His crucifixion? (John 17)

2. How did our Great High Priest, the Messiah, institute the New Covenant in terms of *blood*? (Matthew 26:26-28, Hebrews 9:12)

3. When Jesus gave up His life, He cried out, "It is finished!" (John 19:30) *What* was finished?

4. What sign did God give in the Temple, at the moment of the Messiah's death? (Mark 15:38) (See Hebrews 10:19-20.)

5. What is Jesus' present work for us? (Hebrews 7:25; 9:24)

⟹ **After Jesus' resurrection and ascension to heaven**, the Spirit of God revealed even more about His being the reality to whom the Tabernacle had pointed. Look at Old Testament "shadows" seen in the light of Christ's reality as explained in the letter to the Hebrews, the community steeped in the Old Testament. "Better" is the key word in

Hebrews. *Absorb these "betters"*:

> ➤ "A better covenant" – Hebrews 8:6-7; 9:15
>
> ➤ "Better blood" substituted than animals' – Hebrews 9:25-26
>
> ➤ "Better sanctification" at the laver – Hebrews 2:11
>
> ➤ "A better priest" at the Tabernacle – Hebrews 4:14 to 5:3
>
> ➤ "A better priesthood" – Hebrews 7:11-17
>   (Compare Hebrews 7:1-10 with Genesis 14:18-20.)
>
> ➤ "A better intercessor" at the altar of incense – Hebrews 7:25
>
> ➤ "A better result," finished once and for all – Hebrews 9:24-26
>
> ➤ "A better Tabernacle," the perfect one – Hebrews 8:1-5; 9:1

The Tabernacle expands our realization of sinful man's estrangement from a holy God, and our need to avail ourselves of His provision for our salvation. When the time arrived for the New Covenant to be inaugurated by a "will" activated by the death of the Testator (Hebrews 9:16-22), the Tabernacle system could be laid to rest. Having made the final sacrifice, our Lord provides for the believing sinner's cleansing and moves him or her into service as members of the priesthood of believers. They may even approach the Throne of Grace with boldness, claiming the merit of the Lamb's sacrifice!

IN SUMMARY, JESUS IS THE ULTIMATE AND FINAL GREAT HIGH PRIEST!

The Scriptures present the risen Christ as our one and only mediator between God and man (I Timothy 2:5). The Old Testament "picture book" shows us what was involved in being the Great High Priest of the Tabernacle. Not only did Jesus fulfill that crucial role, He fulfilled all aspects of the Tabernacle's careful pattern. He WAS the lamb, the sanctifier, the light, the bread, the intercessor, the law-keeper, the Mercy Seat. He was, and He IS!

♥ **Here are 5 precious "S's" for the seeker's heart**: When you recognize yourself as a **sinner** and accept the Lamb's **sacrifice** for your own sins, God **sanctifies** you, calls you into **service** in the priesthood of believers (I Peter 2:4-9 and Revelation 1:5-6; 5:10), accepts you at the Mercy Seat (Hebrews 10:19-22), and the result is **satisfaction** for Him and for you! Because He loves us, God has intricately revealed how to come into fellowship with Him, both in shadow and then in reality.

♥ *Which of the five steps have I taken?*

If I belong to the New Covenant "priesthood of believers," how does the Old Covenant enrich my understanding of my amazing role and privilege?

Prayer: *Dear Father, realizing the way You have made into your Presence, I rejoice! I can come boldly through Jesus' new and living way! Amazing!*

Ω

Hold on to the PRIEST KEY to both Covenants!

When Christ came as high priest of the good things that are already here, he went through the greater and more perfect tabernacle that is not man-made, that is to say, not a part of this creation. He did not enter by means of the blood of goats and calves; but he entered the Most Holy Place once for all by his own blood, having obtained eternal redemption.

Hebrews 9:11-12

Study 8

HOST

Who appoints the seasons of our lives?

(Drawn largely from Exodus, Leviticus, Numbers, Deuteronomy)

Introduction: We have seen God's creation of *sacred space* in the study on the Tabernacle. What does His *sacred time* look like? Jewish scholar Abraham Heschel calls Judaism "a religion of Time." From Genesis onward, we find His calendar is built on sevens – seven days, seven years, 7 x 7 + 1 for the Jubilee year, seven articles in the Tabernacle, seven feasts, and repeated sevens in Revelation.

What were feasts for? *(See Study 6 for an outline of the feasts.)* This study on the Messiah as our *host* will look at the feasts' role in the past and then amplify their meaning in terms of Jesus' present and future relationship to them. How did they start? "Three times a year you are to celebrate a festival to me," God specified, calling all males to attend. (See Exodus 23:14 and 17.) "His appointed times" included a renewal of the Covenant with Him, sacrificial worship, teaching, fellowship, and feasting. These celebrations were ideal times to transfer history, commands, principles, symbols, and rituals to the next generation. All five senses were involved, making the experiences highly memorable. Imagine the crowds, the animals, the Temple ceremonies, the blast of the *shofar*, the call of trumpets, the voices of choirs, and the aroma of roasting meat. Understanding the context of a feast can bring a Biblical passage alive.

How did God's feasts fit into human experience? Having created Time, God also set up His calendar of the year. Feasts were carefully timed in relationship to the agricultural seasons, and usually were enjoyed at full moon. Three of the seven were consecutive in spring, one in early summer, and three together in fall. The feasts were focused on Himself and His gifts — the King of the Universe *hosting* His people with the fruit of the vine, the fruit of the field, and the meat of the sacrifices. Praise and joy were fitting responses! Feasts speak of *fellowship.*

⇐ **Context:** The feast patterns were laid out to Moses at Mt. Sinai soon after the Exodus, nearly 1400 years before Christ. Pivotal times in Israel's history are tied to the feasts, such as when the Passover was celebrated on entering the Promised Land (Joshua 5); the Feast of Tabernacles at Solomon's dedication of the first Temple (I Kings 8:2); and when the altar was rebuilt in the Second Temple period (Ezra 3:4, and Nehemiah 8). The feasts were celebrated over the years in wavering states of faithfulness and unfaithfulness. Great feasts were recorded during the reigns of Solomon, Josiah, and Hezekiah, for instance. Carelessness and outright idolatry marked feasts during most of the Divided Kingdom period. When His people went astray, God was grieved with their insincerity. Through the prophets, He said He detested their false ceremonies. The Messiah Himself angrily cleared out the Temple at the beginning and end of His earthly ministry. (John 2:12-16, Luke 19:45-48)

FEAST SUMMARY: *(Shown on pages 56-59)*

(Exodus 23:14-17, Leviticus 23, 25, Numbers 28, 29, Deuteronomy 16)

SPRING: 1. Passover 2. Unleavened Bread 3. First Fruits

SUMMER: 4. Feasts of Weeks (7 weeks + I day after First Fruits) or "Pentecost"

FALL: 5. Trumpets 6. Day of Atonement 7. Tabernacles or "Ingathering"

7th YEAR: Rest for the land, and 50th YEAR: Jubilee

As an example of how seriously God took disobedience to His feast commands, look at the connection between Israel's failure to keep the 7th year fallow land rule for 490 years, and God's judgment. They spent the 70 missed years in captivity in Babylon! It is electrifying to compare Leviticus 25's Jubilee commands with Daniel 9:2's timing, informed by Jeremiah's prophecy in 29:10. II Chronicles 36:21 confirms this "repayment."

⇓ **When Jesus was on earth, He interacted with the feasts** and employed them as platforms for reaching the Covenant community. He used the rituals, symbols, and timing of the feasts to magnify His message and call Israel to realize by Whom they were being visited. (A marvelous resource describing Jesus' interaction with the feasts is found in Alfred Edersheim's classic text, *The Life and Times of Jesus the Messiah*.)

Look at these examples, becoming aware of each festival's atmosphere and spiritual meaning as you explore the feasts:

7th FEAST: Jesus revealing His identity at the Feast of Tabernacles: John 7:2, 14, 37-38

1-3rd FEAST: Jesus Passion week recorded in the Gospels. Examples: Luke 22:7-8

John 12:1, 23-24; 13:1

Matthew 26:17-29

Jesus revealed His fulfillment of the Passover by being the Lamb of God pictured all those years. At the Passover meal on the night before His crucifixion, He instituted "the new covenant in my blood." (Matthew 26:26-28, I Corinthians 11:23-26) He called the unleavened bread "my body given for you." The Old Covenant's provisional sacrifice of the lamb was now being brought to a close by the true Lamb, in accordance with God's valuation of His own Son's blood! The calendar wheeled so significantly from the date of the Messiah's cross and resurrection, that time has been marked as "BC or AD" since that juncture. God's covenants with man progressed from the Old Covenant with Abraham's family, to the New Covenant with all believers in the entire world, whether Jew or Gentile.

4th FEAST: ⟹ 50 days after the Messiah's Passover, the gift of the Holy Spirit was poured out on the believers on the exact date of the 4th feast, *Shavuot,* or the Feast of Weeks ("Pentecost" in Greek). That world-changing event is recorded in Acts 2.

In Acts, the Letters, and Revelation, the Spirit uses "feast" language. The book of Hebrews especially deepens the Old Covenant community's understanding of *Yeshua's* fulfillment of everything the Tabernacle and Feasts foreshadowed.

Look at these passages (all in _past_ tense) that reflect Jesus' ministry in terms of the first four feasts:

Passover: I Peter 1:18-19

Unleavened Bread: I Corinthians 5:7-8

First Fruits: I Corinthians 15:20, 23

Feast of Weeks (Pentecost): Acts 2:14-39, especially verse 33

NOTICE that First Fruits and Feast of Weeks occurred on Sundays. The Resurrection and Pentecost both happened on "the first day of the week" — which may be significant in explaining why the Church worships on that day.

"Completed **in Christ" has been the conclusion to most elements of our study of the Old Covenant.** The feasts are in a different category, in that they do <u>not</u> <u>all</u> seem to be "completed."

Which are and which are not fulfilled? The New Testament records the Messiah's completion of the three Spring Feasts and the fourth, at the beginning of Summer. To reiterate, at the exact week of the Passover, He gave His blood as the sacrificial lamb. His sinless body, "the Bread of life," was broken and buried the evening of the feast of Unleavened Bread. He came forth from the grave the exact day of First-Fruits that year. Exactly 50 days later at the Feast of Weeks, He poured out the Holy Spirit upon all believers, male and female, Jew and Gentile. Those four feasts appear to have been completed on the exact dates that matched God's calendar — impossible timing unless God ordained! On the basis of all these careful fulfillments, it is not unreasonable to expect the last three to match His calendar as well.

The Feasts give us keys to the eschatological significance of God's revelation in terms of process and timing. They give clues to future things that God has promised to complete. Jesus, Prophet of all prophets, promised His second "appearing" on earth. His Spirit continued to inspire prophecy in the New Testament. (See the Feast reference pages 56-57.)

Look at these samples of teaching related to our "blessed hope" – all presented as <u>future</u> expectations:

Trumpets: Paul to Gentiles in I Corinthians 15:51-52 and
  I Thessalonians 4:14-18

Day of Atonement: Written to Jewish believers, in Hebrews 9:7, 28

Ingathering: Revelation 7:9-10

While waiting for Scripture's "blessed hope" to be actualized, Jesus commissioned the Church to reach the world. His "seed," planted in death, was not to "remain alone." In some mysterious way the Church, as well as Israel, are part of God's eternal plan. Meanwhile Israel remains the clock and geo-center of history around which world events still spin today. *Yeshua* asked His people to keep the New Covenant feast (the Lord's Supper) "until I come."

⇔ **When will He "come"?** One clue may be related to God's calendar. Where are we in the process of His fulfillment of the Biblical feasts? Their progressive nature helps us sense something of their eschatological timing and significance. The feasts are like the drama of the ages being played out in seven acts. Unfinished aspects appear in "shadow form" until they happen. It is natural to wonder where we are on God's timeline. We can be sure that God will keep His promises. The Messiah is the marker. Since we trust in God's promises, we can be confident that eventually "the times <u>will</u> have reached their fulfillment," as we are assured in Ephesians 1:9-10:

> And he made known to us the mystery of his will according to his good pleasure, which he purposed in Christ, to be put into effect <u>when the times will have reached their fulfillment</u> – to bring all things in heaven and on earth together under one head, even Christ.

What about the Fall Feasts? The 5th – Trumpets, the 6th – Day of Atonement, and the 7th – Ingathering, seem to be yet unfulfilled. They point toward "closure time." Consider that trumpets may be used to announce either judgment or joy at the great Ingathering. (That seventh feast, Ingathering, is also called the Feast of Tabernacles, and was foreseen in Zechariah 14:16.)

What is Feast 6 about? Between the Feast of Trumpets (5th) and the Ingathering (7th) is the mysterious day of the 6th feast. Actually, it is not a day of feasting, but of *fasting*. It is called "the Day of Atonement."

Leviticus 16 prescribes it and Hebrews 9 rehearses the events of that Day, pointing out the Messiah's completion of the Atonement. So in what sense might we think of this "Day" as <u>un</u>fulfilled? On that Day, ancient Israel stood at attention, waiting for the High Priest to emerge from the earthly Tabernacle, assuring them that God had accepted the atoning blood. Our Great High Priest has entered the heavenly Tabernacle, but has not yet emerged. Hebrews 9:24 and 28 put it this way:

> For Christ did not enter a man-made sanctuary that was only a copy of the true one; he entered heaven itself, now to appear for us in God's presence.
> ...so Christ was sacrificed once to take away the sins of many people, and he will appear a second time, not to bear sin, but to bring salvation to those who are waiting for him.

How might this give us a clue about the 6th feast? This mysterious day of fasting may be related to unbelieving Israel's recognition of their true Messiah's atonement. To realize "whom they have pierced" would bring anguish. *Consider these the implications of these four Scriptures, taken together:*

John 19:36-37

Zechariah 12:10

Psalm 22:16

Revelation 1:7

Some unbelieving Israelites wait. Some Jewish people still look for a coming Messiah, but most seem blinded to His having come. (See "the veil" in II Corinthians 3:13-14.)

Jewish believers in *Yeshua* expectantly wait for the Messiah's return. Today's growing Messianic Movement is challenging Israel's unbelieving majority. They have long assumed they could not believe in "the Gentiles' Jesus" — the Jesus they assume represents Christendom's treatment of their people. Thankfully, those who have awakened to His identity are moving forward in the train of the Ist Century believers who were nearly all Jewish. They look forward to the restoration of Israel, counting on the Prophets' predictions that the "olive tree" will bud again. The Scriptures promise that there are still good things ahead for the "root" into which believing Gentiles are engrafted "branches." While Paul was called to be the Apostle to the Gentiles, his three chapters in Romans 9, 10, and 11 hold out great hope for Israel.

Until He returns, Jesus hosts all His people (Jew or Gentile) at two kinds of feasts right now. *Ponder over these feasts and consider the depth of experience each offers the believer:*

I Corinthians 11:23-26:
  This Feast is called _____

  It looks back to _____ and toward what _____

Revelation 3:19-20:
  What would you call this "feast"? _____

  To whom is it offered? _____ How often? _____

At the climax of history, an altogether new celebration appears in Revelation 19:7-9. *The Bridal Feast stands as a beacon in the future:*

This feast's name is _____

Who will be there? _____

We can barely grasp the wonder, awe, and joy that will attend this future feast. Even our own human feasts mark some deeply meaningful past event or initiate some new beginning. The Marriage Feast of the Lamb will mark the end of the Fall's ravages, and the beginning of a whole new life!

Those who have received Jesus as the Suffering Servant at His first coming wait eagerly for His second appearance (Hebrews 9:28). The next time, He will come as the Bridegroom King. Who could be more thrilled than the Lamb's Bride?

♥ *How do I feel about His "appearing"?*

A special "crowning" awaits those who have longed for His return.

> Now there is in store for me the crown of righteousness which the Lord, the righteous Judge, will award to me on that day — and not only to me, but also to all who have longed for his appearing.
>
> II Timothy 4:8

Prayer: *Father, may your Spirit indwelling me give me a passion for your Son's return. May I joyfully anticipate sitting down with you at the Marriage Feast, for your Word says, "No eye has seen, no ear has heard, no mind has conceived what God has prepared for those who love him."*

Ω

Hold on to the HOST KEY to both Covenants!

⚷

For Christ our Passover lamb has been sacrificed. Therefore let us keep the Festival, not with the old yeast, the yeast of malice and wickedness, but with bread without yeast, the bread of sincerity and truth.

I Corinthians 5:7b-8

Study 9
KING

Who was destined to be King? How does that process relate to my destiny?

(Drawn largely from the historical and prophetic books)

Introduction: In the *Torah* (first 5 books of the Old Testament), we have seen the Messiah prefigured as the *2nd Adam*, the *Son of the promise* to Abraham, the *Lamb of God*, and as the reality to whom the *Tabernacle* and *Feasts* pointed. Moses acted as mediator between God and the people, and the Levitical priesthood acted as Israel's representatives before God. (See Exodus 19:3-8.) Studies 9 and 10 move on to the rest of the Old Testament. The background scene changes from Abraham's pilgrimage, the Egyptian bondage, and the wilderness wanderings, to Israel's entrance into the Promised Land under Joshua in the 1300's BC, and the eventual establishment of the Monarchy.

Context: What are the rest of the Old Testament books about? This period could be seen as "experiments in human government." After Joshua, various judges loosely ruled Israel 400 years. Going on with the 1st and 2nd books of Samuel, Kings, and Chronicles, we watch Israel becoming a nation in the Promised Land. God has been their King. When they cry for "a king like the nations" (I Samuel 12), God allows them their desire, but the results are repeatedly disastrous, reign after reign. Led by kings who are often corrupted, Israel is sent prophets, who represent God to the people. Saul, David, and Solomon rule the Kingdom at its high point, during which the stationary Temple is built in Jerusalem in about 950 BC, replacing the movable Tabernacle. From that "golden age" we have David's Psalms and Solomon's writings. After Solomon's death, the Monarchy breaks into two Divided Kingdoms, the Southern one called "Judah" and the Northern called "Israel." Recurring periods of apostasy, repentance, reform, decay, idolatry, and judgment, are chronicled from about the 900's through the 400's BC.

Into this record of unfaithfulness God injects the burden of His heart through His chosen prophets. He gives them a message for their times, always prefaced with, "Thus saith the Lord." God's loving guidance, correction, and discipline echo through these wandering generations. In spite of great failures, hope shines through the prophets' messages, hope for Israel's restoration and for a coming Messiah.

⇐ **Two "shepherd kings":** Both King David and the Messianic King understood that God was the King of Israel, and that they were to be shepherds of His people. "Yours is the Kingdom," David prayed in I Chronicles 29:11. To him was given God's promise of an ongoing reign of the "Son of David" (II Samuel 7:8-17). We see the Messianic King prefigured in many of David's meditations, such as Psalm 72. The Savior applies them to Himself when He comes to earth. (Example: Psalm 110:1 appealed to in Matthew 22:41-46 and cross references in Mark and Luke.)

The "messianic hope": The prophets were sometimes given glimpses of Israel's future time of restoration and glory. Their previews spoken across the centuries point to a coming figure that appears in various forms. Biblical passages that foreshadow a final Deliverer are called "messianic." That is, they point to God's ultimate Messiah, meaning "the Anointed One." This figure is mysterious, for sometimes He appears as a *triumphant king* in victory, and at other times, as a *suffering servant*, in apparent defeat. *Notice the different tone of these two Psalms:*

Psalm 2

Psalm 22

⇓ **What are we to make of the Messiah's differing roles** prefigured in these Psalms' opposite movements? Remember that the devastation of the Fall had held the world in subjection to "the ruler of this world." Jesus understood His redemptive mission well, and repeatedly tried to prepare His disciples for the paradox of His mysterious assignments.

How clearly did Jesus predict His death? Here are examples:

Mark 8:31-32

Mark 10:32-34

The Son of God knew that there was no other way to pay for the redemption of the human race except through the death of the perfect Lamb of God. And so in His first coming, *Yeshua* lived out the role of the sacrificial lamb of Isaiah 53, with the words of Psalm 22 on His lips. *What aspects of the Messiah's experience does Isaiah 53 describe?*

The messianic mystery: The Messiah knew that His resurrection was coming, that He would return to the Father (John 17:1-5, 13) and that the Son of Man would eventually return to earth in glory (Matthew 16:27). But He knew that His saving work had to be accomplished first. (Matthew 20:28)

Biblical expectation and popular expectation often differed. The popular expectation of the Messiah in the 1st century was of a "Son of David" who would be a conqueror and would free Israel from Rome.

(John 7:42) How could they accept an obviously less-than- triumphant Messiah? They could not recognize *Yeshua* to be the "king of glory" of David's Psalm 24:7.

Corroboration is the Biblical way God proves the Messianic King's identity. The Spirit of God gave <u>details</u> of the Messiah's life through the prophets. These details would have to match the life of the contender for the Kingly title. One necessity was the Messiah's relationship to King David. An argument at the feast recorded in John 7:42 turns around the Scripture (Micah 5:2) that said the Christ must come from David's family and from Bethlehem. Jesus' enemies were not aware that Jesus of Nazareth matched that clue. (Matthew 1:1; 2:1-2, 5)

See how Jesus handled an argument with the Pharisees over messianic Psalm 110, involving Solomon: (Matthew 22:41-45)

Who had Jesus called Himself in relation to Solomon? (Matthew 12:42)

Yeshua spoke humbly, but told the truth. The Messiah's <u>identity</u> keeps being the issue. Unless He was truly who He claimed to be, He could not be authentic. If He were not God in the flesh, He could not accomplish the God-sized task of redeeming mankind.

⇓ **What kind of Kingdom was God initiating** through His Son's arrival on earth? Jesus said the Kingdom was "at hand" (Matthew 4:17, RSV). Apparently His contemporaries largely missed His message. However, we live after the Messiah's vindication by His rising from the dead. We have been given the teaching of the Holy Spirit after the Resurrection and can reassess what Jesus was communicating. We can ponder some of His teachings, parables, rebuttals, and predictions that were related to His authority, the Kingdom, and His Kingship.

⇓ **For instance, Jesus' prophetic voice was often veiled in parables.** Parables spoke in a unique way that fitted what was necessary – so that the "hearing" would hear, and the "deaf" would not.

What do we "hear" in parables like the following two – now that we know the end of the story?

Matthew 22:1-14 – The wedding of the King's son:

Matthew 25:1-13 – The parable of the ten virgins:

Jesus looked into the future and gave us a preview of what to expect as the world approaches the end of Time and beginning of Eternity. Although it is a long passage, it is wise to read Matthew 24 and 25 through at one sitting, to face the reality of what the world faces in the future — perhaps the near future. *Yeshua* revealed these things in His last week, between Palm Sunday and the night of the Lord's Supper. Jesus begins to foretell Jerusalem's imminent destruction (Luke 19:41-44), and what to expect eventually, at the end of the age.

What kind of things will happen before the end comes?
        Matthew 24:4-14

How much power does the Messianic King have? Matthew 26:53-54

Who will judge the world, and on what basis? Matthew 25:31-46

How much authority has been given to the risen Christ, the Messianic Son? Matthew 28:18

↓ **A few decades after His resurrection, Jesus is revealed** to the Apostle John in the opening of Revelation as the Lamb-become-Lion being worshipped in heaven (Revelation 5:5-14). As the Apocalypse deepens, He is declared to be both Lord and Christ (Revelation 11:15-19). His name is KING OF KINGS AND LORD OF LORDS (Revelation 19:16). At the close of the message, He calls Himself "the Root and Offspring of David" (Revelation 22:16) — soon coming for His bride (Revelation 22:20). What majesty! May these passages deepen our worship and expectation.

✺ *Reality check! The Son of God did not come to set up a temporary kingdom in a little Middle Eastern nation. He was bringing in a Kingdom for all peoples that spanned all time and space, from earth to heaven!*

We strain to even imagine the climax of the world's history. J.R.R. Tolkien's *Lord of the Rings* comes to its climax in *The Return of the King*. The allegorical kingdom was languishing. Most of its subjects had lost hope but a few still waited for their rightful king to return. How much more our poor fallen race is languishing without hope. What joy will herald the return of the only rightful King of God's beloved world!

How shall I apply the claims of Christ's kingdom to myself?

Does Eternity seem too nebulous to care about in Time? What if, as C.S. Lewis put it, "Life on earth is just the preface to the book"?

♥ *To which king and kingdom do I make my choice to belong in Time, and therefore in Eternity?*

Prayer: *Yes, Lord Jesus, I echo the words of I Timothy 1:17, "Now to the King eternal, immortal, invisible, the only God, be honor and glory for ever and ever! Amen!"*

Ω

Hold on to the KING KEY to both Covenants!

8—⚲

"I, Jesus, have sent my angel to give you this testimony for the churches. I am the Root and the Offspring of David, and the bright Morning Star."

Revelation 22:16

Study 10

PROPHET

Who was the ultimate 'prophet to come'?

(Drawn from the historical books and a wide spectrum of Scriptures)

Introduction: The calling of a prophet was to speak for God, prefacing his words with, "Thus saith the Lord." Christ used no such personal disclaimer. "I say," was His direct statement, reflecting the profound prerogative of deity. Human prophets spoke _for_ God, but the Christ spoke _as_ God. The true <u>prophet</u>'s office served the nation like "checks and balances" to <u>kings</u> and <u>priests</u>. The Messiah fulfills all three roles. Scripture shows Him to be God's ultimate priest, prophet, and king.

Context: Between Moses and Jesus, God raised up many prophets to speak to the Hebrews. Although they had asked for a king, and God had allowed it, the rest of the Old Testament chronicles a "leanness of soul" to which the prophets spoke. The office of prophet was actually above that of king. Prophets anointed, encouraged, corrected, and warned the king. They sometimes censured the priests. They revealed God's perspective – sometimes metaphorically – to the nation. Even with pronouncements of judgment, hope shines through. Basically, prophets were _forth-tellers_. Sometimes they were _fore-tellers_ of events soon to happen, or glimpsed in the far future.

⇐ **We hear God's heart in passages from the prophets.** These men suffered greatly to represent God before recalcitrant kings and priests and often unfaithful people – much as we are. We are brought up short as we hear Nathan rebuke David, or hear Hosea echo God's broken heart. We see God's power at work in the lives of Elijah, Elisha, Isaiah, and Jeremiah. The anguish of God heard through the prophets grips our hearts.

⇐ **Let us ponder the role of prophecy.** *What were the prophets searching for, as the Spirit gave them utterance?*

I Peter 1:10-12

II Peter 1:20-21

⇔ **A prophetic key: "The Elijah" clue spans both Testaments.** The Old Testament (in the Christian Old Testament order) ends with the promise of a prophet called "the Elijah." (Malachi 4:5; 3:1) After 400 years with no prophetic voice, the New Testament begins with a prophet speaking again. (Luke 3:1-3) John the Baptist was both the last Old Covenant prophet, and the forerunner of the Messiah. Jesus explains that John is "the Elijah," in Matthew 11:14. It was John the Baptist who identified Jesus to the crowds: "Behold the Lamb of God!"

Authentication **is one of God's methods of certifying truth and revealing identity.** Messianic prophecy in the Old Testament points to the identity of the Son. All the prophecies are summed up in Him, as *Yeshua* explained on the Emmaus road. Jesus fulfilled detail after detail of the messianic prophecies. What are the odds of anyone other than Jesus matching all the specifications of the foreshadowed Messiah? *Here are a few that had to be verified:*

➢ His Humanity – Genesis 3:15 and Luke 3:37-38; 19:10

➢ His family – Genesis 12:1-3; 22:15-18 and Matthew1:1-17

➢ His tribe – Genesis 49:10 and Luke 2:4

➢ The time of His appearing – Daniel 9:24-26 and Luke 2:1- 2

➢ His birthplace – Micah 5:2 and Matthew 2:1-6

➢ His reception and death – Isaiah 53, John 12:38, and Acts 8:32-35

➢ His resurrection – Genesis 22:1-19, John 8:56, Hebrews 11:17-19, along with the four Gospels' resurrection accounts.

⇐ ⇓ **"Are you the Prophet?" they asked Jesus.** God had promised a prophet to succeed Moses, an ultimate prophet. (Deuteronomy 18:15-18; Acts 7:37) Jesus was both the subject of prophecy and was that promised prophet. In His case, "the media IS the message."

See how Peter and Stephen applied Moses' prophecy, soon after the outpouring of the Spirit at Pentecost:

Acts 3:17-26

Acts 7:37 (quoting Deuteronomy 18:15)

Jesus' prophetic authenticity was put to the test. His prophecies became starkly actualized. "Coming true" was the test of true prophecy according to Deuteronomy 18:22. *Here are examples:*

He would be the suffering servant of Isaiah 53 – Luke 22:37

His disciples would betray, deny, and defect – John 13:21, 38; 16:32

He would be crucified and rise on the third day – Matthew 16:21 (also recorded in Mark 8:31, Luke 9:22, Luke 18:33.)

Jerusalem would be demolished — unthinkable at the time —Luke 19:41-44. (The Temple was destroyed in 70 AD, 40 years later.)

$\Rightarrow$ **Some of the Messiah's prophecies stated on earth** wait for final fulfillment. On the basis of Jesus' proven prophetic reliability, these predictions are confidently expected, awesome as they are:

The final tribulation – Matthew 24:15-29

His return and gathering of the elect – Matthew 24:30-31, 36-50

The final judgment – Matthew 25:31-46

$\Rightarrow$ **Jesus' disciples' confident message** was based on two factors: prophetic fulfillments and the Resurrection's vindication of the Son's identity. These early sermons are a treasure. *Note key verses in each that appeal to prophetic fulfillments or to the Resurrection:*

At Pentecost: Acts 2:1-36, note verses 24, 31-32

To the Sanhedrin: Acts 4:8-12, note verse 10

At Stephen's defense: Acts 7:1-56, note verse 56

On to Gentile Cornelius in Israel: Acts 10:34-43, note verse 40

On to Gentiles in Psidian Antioch, Asia, Acts 13:16-41, note verse 30

Their message was to be given the Spirit's empowerment. (Acts 1:8) The night before the Cross, Jesus prepared them to receive the One who would replace Him. *How did He say the Holy Spirit's location would change?*

Especially see the prepositions in John 14:16-17.

Jesus' Replacement arrives: At the Feast of Pentecost 50 days after Jesus' resurrection, the Holy Spirit was poured out on earth! (Acts 2) The Incarnation had made God visible in the face of Jesus Christ. (II Corinthians 4:6) Now the Spirit would make Him palpable in the hearts of His people. From Jesus' Ascension to His Enthronement in heaven marked a 10-day pause between two amazing happenings in the 1st Century — first "God with us," and then "God in us"!

Prophecy continues: After the Incarnation, the Spirit of Christ continued to inspire the writing of documents that became the New Testament. *What specific expectations do you find in these passages?*

♦ All nations to be reached – Romans 16:26

♦ The return of Christ – I Thessalonians 4:16-17

♦ Judgment on the earth – II Corinthians 5:10;
     Romans 14:10-12

♦ After judgment, a new heaven and earth – II Peter 3:10-13

♦ The handing over of the Kingdom – I Corinthians 15:24

↓ **Later, Jesus in the book of Revelation opened an awesome door into the future.** A voice tells John, "Come up here, and I will show you what must take place after this" (Revelation 4:1b). We glimpse the final cataclysms and judgments in chapters 6-20, and can ponder what these final events will mean for humanity.

Various clues are given about final resolutions that inspire great joy. *Try to imagine these stages of fulfillment of the blessed hope of those written in "the Lamb's book of life" (Revelation 21:27):*

Every tribe and nation represented at the throne – Revelation 5:9

The rule of the Messiah – Revelation 11:15

The marriage of the Lamb – Revelation 19:7

The new heaven and new earth glimpsed – Revelation 21:1

The promised coming of Christ for His Bride – Revelation 22:7

Do prophecy-honoring believers trust fact or fiction? Bottom line, they trust the ultimate Prophet, the Messiah, to keep His word. Believing Jesus to be who He is, they trust that what He says will yet come to pass. The *Son of man's* first appearance as the *Lamb* provided redemption and fulfilled the prophets' shadowy clues. The *Son of God's* second appearance, finally as *King*, will assuredly bring in the reality of the Kingdom. (Hebrews 9:26-28)

The great climax before the Beginning: We might think that the 2000 years of waiting seems to be either a hopelessly long forgetting, or a faith-shattering silence from God. Remember that the Hebrew pilgrimage from Abraham to the Messiah took 2000 years, too.

Consider these affirmations that the Spirit of God has given us:

♦ The reason for His lingering: II Peter 3:9

♦ God's time measurement: II Peter 3:8

♦ God's faithfulness: I Thessalonians 5:24

♦ Unable to be separated from His love: Romans 8:31-39

♦ The goal He will accomplish: Ephesians 1:9-10

♦ The Church's role in fulfillment: Matthew 24:14

In Matthew 24, the disciples asked, "What will be the sign of your coming and the end of the age?" The Prophet of all prophets could predict warning signs, but He could not tell us WHEN! *What does Matthew 24:36 say about Who knows? What is the Savior's "therefore" advice in the meantime, in verse 42?*

How seriously should we take messianic promises in the 21ˢᵗ Century? Since God is reliable, we today can count upon the actualization of unfulfilled prophecies. Many Scriptures help us think this through.

♥ *Early Christians were told to "comfort each other with these words" (I Thessalonians 4:18). Do I need this comfort?*

♥ In a world rife with hate, war, disease, and misery, do I need assurance that God will bring in the benediction of His Kingdom? (Rev. 21:3-5; 22:20)

♥ As instructed in Hebrews 12:1-3, 11, and prayed for in Colossians 1:9-14, do I need patience to receive God's promise?

♥ In light of Matthew 6:10 and 24:14, do I have a significant purpose in relation to the coming of the Kingdom?

♥ In light of the Messianic King's appeal to the seven churches in Revelation 2 and 3, am I purposing to overcome?

Prayer: *Oh Lord, I ask your Spirit's help to embrace the assurance of your eternal purpose. May He work patience and perseverance in my life as I look to the Son in these seemingly last days.*

Ω

Hold on to the PROPHET KEY to both Covenants!

In the past God spoke to our forefathers through the prophets at many times and in various ways, but in these last days he has spoken to us by his Son, whom he appointed heir of all things, and through whom he made the universe. The Son is the radiance of God's glory and the exact representation of his being, sustaining all things by his powerful word.

Hebrews 1:1-3a

Study II

ALL

Who qualifies as 'all in all'?

(Drawn from the whole Bible, panoramically)

Introduction: ALL started with Christ's challenge to those on the road to Emmaus, in Luke 24:25-27. When they realized who the Stranger was, they ran back to tell the others huddled in Jerusalem.

Look at what happened later that Sunday night (Luke 24:36-49), and imagine that you had been one of them. Think about these questions:

Q. How did you feel about Jesus being alive, showing you His wounds, and eating fish in front of you?

Q. When He appealed to the prophecies, and you realized some aspects had just been completed, what did He say would come next?

Q. When He said, "I am going to send you what my Father has promised," what did you anticipate?

Context: Some time later (recorded in John 21 and Matthew 28:16-20) Jesus is meeting with them in Galilee. Then at the end of the 40 days, at His Ascension (Luke 24:50-52 and Acts 1:1-11), they are told to stay in Jerusalem, wait to be "baptized with the Holy Spirit," and then go forth on an astounding assignment.

Q. What do you think you would be feeling or expecting, as those days of waiting lingered on, and the crowds poured into Jerusalem for the next feast?

Might you have been overwhelmed by your assigned task, knowing that the authorities who had killed *Yeshua* at the last feast wanted His eye-witnesses dead too? Might you be asking yourself, *"How? How can our little band ever launch the ambassadorship our Lord Jesus assigned us? Some miracle, some divine leadership, some new power would have to appear — something like what happened at the Lord's resurrection!"*

That is exactly what did happen, as recorded in Acts I. On the 50th day after First Fruits, the Spirit of God made as significant an entrance into the world as the Messiah had at His Incarnation. As Jesus had told them (John 7:37-39, and 14:17), the Spirit would be changing His relationship from being "with" them, to being "in" them. On the day of Pentecost, He came upon each of the individual believers. The Spirit manifested His Presence by fire on their heads and the message of redemption on their lips — heard in all the languages of the pilgrims to Jerusalem!

Although the frightened band of disciples had felt impotent, the Spirit launched the "mission impossible" in Jerusalem with power, signs, and wonders that only God could accomplish. As they followed along, they discovered the Spirit was as real a Presence as the

Incarnate Christ's. Furthermore, He could be with — no, <u>in</u> — each of them at the same time — and also in us who would come after them!

Now, how can we gather our studies' gains together? Along with the first believers, we have been given a myriad of clues about God's purposes from Jesus' own mouth and from the Spirit's teachings. How can we hold on to these insights? Among many ways, three to explore might be these:

> *A.* *Examining interactive Scriptures* – when we look back and forth between related biblical references for amplification.

> *B.* *Grasping a progressive view point* – when we try to see the Bible as a panoramic whole, historically.

> *C.* *Clarifying and correcting relational concepts* – when we focus on the intertwined relationships between the Old and New Covenant revelations, and between the Old and New Covenant communities.

Examining interactive Scriptures (*A*), let's use the chart on the next page combining Messianic roles focused on in *ALL* listing Old and New Testament Scriptures for comparison and contrast. When we understand the earlier Covenant's basis of each of these typological roles in the Old Testament, they fill the New Testament account of Jesus' identities full of meaning. "What was concealed in the Old is revealed in the New." Furthermore, both Testaments become richer in meaning if we understand both their proclamation and their actualization. The two Covenants work like mirrors that reveal things back and forth that would not be seen as they stood alone.

Don't let a "chart" form dull your spirit. On the next page's chart, jot in "remembering" phrases (memory helps) under the key passages listed on the Messianic Roles chart.

♥ *Star the ones that stand out to you — through which the Spirit especially enlightens you.*

♥ *Circle the one that you'd most hope to "internalize" and apply to your relationship with the Lord.*

Messianic Roles	Old Testament Keys	New Testament Keys
SEED	Genesis 3:15	I Cor. 15:21-23
SON	Genesis 22:2	Hebrews 11:17-19
LAMB	Exodus 12:6-13	John 1:29
PRIEST	Leviticus 16	Hebrews 9:23-24
HOST	Exodus 23:14-17	Revelation 3:20
KING	II Samuel 7:12-16	Revelation 22:16
PROPHET	Deuteronomy 18:18	Luke 24:25-27

Grasping a progressive view point (*B*) This whole study has been like taking a flying trip over Biblical history, giving the participant a vantage point from above. Landing fields have been indicated (by Scriptures in brackets) where the traveler may go down and scan the landscape more carefully. A panoramic overview helps travelers perceive patterns far below, and glimpse clouds high above.

♥ *In what ways has a "progressive revelation" view of the Bible helped me?*

Clarifying and correcting relational concepts (*C*) The Old Covenant serves as the foundation of God's "house," on which the upper floor of the New Covenant is securely built. God provides an overarching roof over the house of God, one that shelters, protects, strengthens, and gives beauty. The cornerstone is Jesus Christ. The pillars of this structure run from base to roof, through both floors — the Old and New Testament "floors." First God set up the Tabernacle pattern, then Jesus "tabernacled with us," and now the Spirit of God is "tabernacling" in believers. All mankind (i.e., Jews and Gentiles) are invited to become members — "living stones" — in this living tabernacle. Paul told Gentile Christians (Ephesians 2:19-22):

> Consequently, you are no longer foreigners and aliens,
> but fellow citizens with God's people and members
> of God's household, built on the foundation of the
> apostles and prophets, with Christ Jesus himself as
> the chief cornerstone. In him the whole building is
> joined together and rises to become a holy temple in
> the Lord. And in him you too are being built together
> to become a dwelling in which God lives by his Spirit.

These facts explained to the Ephesian church were hard for the Jewish believers to accept, but the matter had been settled by God at Pentecost. At the Jerusalem Council (recorded in Acts 15) the apostolic leadership realized that they had to agree with God.

The inclusion Jesus accomplished has been attacked by Satan very effectively since the Jerusalem Council, turning the two communities against each other. Standing in the gap today, the current Messianic Movement of Jewish believers in *Yeshua* as the Messiah signifies a ray of hope for God's Household to come back together, to His glory.

♥ *How do I see Jewish and Gentile believers any differently than before this study?*

⟸⇓⟹ **After the Incarnation, what was to happen next?** Old "wineskins" + Holy Spirit = a need for new "wineskins"! When we examine the New Testament, we find great upheaval at the point of the Messiah's convergence between the Old and New Covenants. For example, when questioned by the establishment of His day about their tradition of fasting, *Yeshua* answered in Matthew 9:15, 17:

> How can the guests of the bridegroom mourn while he is with them? The time will come when the bridegroom will be taken from them; then they will fast. . . . Neither do men pour new wine into old wineskins. If they do, the skins will burst, the wine will run out and the wineskins will be ruined. No, they pour new wine into new wineskins, and both are preserved.

What were these "new wine and wine skins" of which Jesus spoke? Although in continuity with the past, the Incarnation brought in something altogether new. The New Testament calls it another "mystery." The mystery of the Messiah's identity had finally been solved. Now the mystery of God's eternal plan was unfolding to those with eyes to see, eyes given sight by the gift of the Holy Spirit to believers. Scripture announces this mystery to a Gentile community (Ephesians 3:6):

This mystery is that through the gospel the Gentiles are heirs together with Israel, members together of one body, and sharers together in the promise in Christ Jesus.

Gentiles "heirs with Israel" — the Covenant People? Unthinkable! God's eternal plan includes non-Jews, women, and all nations? The prophets had glimpsed this. Jesus had hinted at it, telling the Pharisees that He had "sheep of other folds" (John 10:16), and telling His disciples this was about to happen (John 16:27-28; 17:20).

⟹ **When did God demonstrate this wineskin-bulging fact to the believing community?** And how? He did it at the next gathering of the Jewish community 50 days after Jesus' resurrection, at the Feast of Weeks. At 9:00 AM (the time of the morning sacrifice in the Temple), the Spirit of God began to proclaim the identity of the risen Lord in all the languages of the pilgrims to the feast. He spoke through the mouths of the believers in whom He had suddenly taken up residence. This gift was poured out as a sign that Jesus had been enthroned in heaven! All Jesus <u>was</u> and <u>is</u> thereafter is made available to all believers — Jew or Gentile, male or female, slave or free. "Come to God at the Temple" suddenly changed to "Go to the world's peoples wherever they are!" Talk about "new wine"! It is all documented in the first chapters of Acts.

⟹⟹**The Incarnation is not over!** The New Covenant community, built on the Old, was operationally transformed by God's outpouring of His Spirit on His people. Jesus had "tabernacled" on earth during the Incarnation. Next, He sent the Spirit to indwell His people as "the body of Christ" on earth. Now the Incarnation continues by means of the Holy Spirit making the Word become flesh in God's people, one by one!

God has provided everything we need IN HIM who has died and risen to give us new life. A transformed life is what the Gospel of the Kingdom of God guides us into. We've only gone part of the way by grasping the Old Testament foundations. Indwelt by the Spirit, we more deeply understand Who Jesus was and is. As we live "in Him," we grow into cooperation with God's goal.

Paul prayed for a revolution of the heart — that "the eyes of your heart may be enlightened" — in Ephesians 1:18 (*a prayer to claim*):

> I pray also that the eyes of your heart may be enlightened in order that you may know the hope to which he has called you, the riches of his glorious inheritance in the saints, and his incomparably great power for us who believe.

Surely, without the Spirit's disclosing truth to us, we sons and daughters of Adam are blind and deaf. The Chinese Bible teacher Watchman Nee asserted in *The Normal Christian Life* (normal, not sub-normal) (on page 101) that, "The revelation of the fact of the Spirit's indwelling can revolutionize the life of any Christian!"

"Indwelling" is the crux of this dynamic of the Holy Spirit. It starts with "in." To reiterate, the Old Covenant and New Covenant key words are *ALL* and *IN*. Christ is proven to <u>be</u> ALL, and <u>is</u> ALL in His people. The Spirit teaches us that everything we need is "in Him."

⇒ ⇒ <u>IN</u> **invites us into the storehouses of God,** disclosed to us by the Spirit. We will find that all the roles of the Messiah that were foreshadowed and then fulfilled are now activated in a new way — new wine in new wineskins! The amazing disclosure is that God has given us transformed relationships in two dimensions — "you in Christ" and "Christ in you." (IN-ness is the focus of $\mathcal{ALL}$'s companion study, $\mathcal{IN}$.)

If I choose to go on now, knowing what I do about ALL, to embrace what it means to be IN, I will be putting myself on the pathway to what the Westminster Catechism calls "the chief end of man" — "knowing God and enjoying Him forever."

♥ *In what ways has my mind or heart been transformed on my Emmaus walk with Jesus?*

Prayer: *Thank you, Father, for how you are changing me, among so many others, as I respond to your ALL in the Messiah! May I trust your Spirit IN me to continue to transform my life increasingly "to the praise of God's glory."*

Ω

Hold on to the" ALL" KEY to both Covenants!

⚿

He said to them, "How foolish you are, and how slow [of heart] to believe all that the prophets have spoken! Did not the Messiah have to suffer these things and then enter his glory?" And beginning with Moses and all the Prophets, he explained to them what was said in all the Scriptures concerning himself.

Luke 24:25-27 (NIV 2011)

Study 12

BRIDEGROOM
In addition to the Messiah's roles foreseen in the original Testament, what new identity is revealed in the New Testament? What does this mean for us today?

(Drawn from the whole Bible, and related to today's situation.)

Introduction to our BRIDEGROOM study: The New Testament's revelation of believers' present and future relationship to the Messiah is thrilling. Before exploring His Bridegroom identity, let's revisit the identities that we have examined in these studies that have been true for centuries. Believers have needed these bedrock understandings through every generation. Signs of their approaching finalizations are multiplying day by day, not just year by year. Let's look back at *ALL*'s studies, seeking to understand how the Messiah's various roles interact with our own generation. We'll need to ask for insight only the Spirit can reveal!

WHO (Identity)

Today people are asking, "Who can deliver us?" Men's hearts are failing them for fear these days. The world is in political turmoil with refugees spilling out over the globe and economic collapses threatening. At times of instability and panic, people are sometimes willing to trade their freedoms and rights for security by accepting a self-proclaimed deliverer. These are dangerous days.

Faith situations over the world are mixed. Blindness to the identity of the Messiah cripples the faltering "reached" Western world, those most without excuse. Yet unreached millions are getting the opportunity to hear about their Savior for the first time. A growing number of the Messiah's own Jewish people are awakening to His identity and proclaiming *Yeshua* to be the true Messiah for the world. Radical Islam is on the march. In our generation, those who claim Him in repressive societies are being persecuted and martyred at an unprecedented rate.

While Jesus was on earth, His *identity* was the most crucial fact that His life, teachings, and miracles were meant to reveal. Matthew 16:15 (also in Mark 8:27-29, Luke 9:18-20) records the moment when the Spirit led Peter to understand that Jesus actually was the long awaited Messiah. But that term to lst Century Israelites tended to mean a Deliverer from Rome, not a Savior of the world. Jesus immediately followed Peter's pronouncement with the prediction of His death. Peter's rebuke put him on the side of Satan's program to de-rail the Savior's work of redemption. The disciples could not yet grasp the fact that the Seed must die, that the Lamb must be sacrificed, and that the Great High Priest must carry His perfect blood of Atonement into Heaven's Temple.

Today we have more evidence of the Messiah's identity than Peter had. During the Incarnation, they had the Old Testament, but no Gospels, Acts, Letters, or Revelation. The Holy Spirit had not yet been sent to indwell those born of God. It is we who are privileged to be able to "put it all together."

♥ *What have I decided to believe about His identity?*

SEED (Redemption)

What are the Messiah's "many seeds" (John 12:24) experiencing in our generation? Looking back to the beginning at what God had pronounced at the Fall (Genesis 3:14-15), the heel of the Seed of Eve eventually was crushed on the Cross and the serpent's head was mortally wounded before his eventual demise. Until the Seed's final triumph, however, the ancient dragon continues to pursue Eve's progeny, as the scene in Revelation 12:13-17 reveals. His people have been hated by the Dragon for centuries, and are still the target of his enmity. Satan manipulates his agents to try to exterminate Israel and pursue Christians who profess faith in Jesus. We see that in shockingly blatant and brutal forms today.

In secularized societies, the fact of the battle that Satan wages against Adam's race is largely forgotten, denied, or never known. Instead of being repulsed as humanity's common enemy, he has succeeded in pitting the world's cultures against each other through struggles for power, wars, ethnic hatreds, and false religions.

What has God's Word said about the "seed"?

What kind of signs from God revealed the arrival of the Seed? Luke 1:26-38, Luke 2:8-15

What goal did the Seed understand would be accomplished through His death? John 12:23-24

How do the seed of Adam and the seed of Christ compare? I Corinthians 15:20-22

♥ *Am I one of His many seeds?*

SON (Origin)

Today the family of Abraham seems locked in perpetual strife. Isaac and Ishmael continue in enmity in the Middle East. When the Son out of Abraham/Isaac/Jacob's family was born on earth and revealed Himself, He was rejected. He died as God's final Lamb, but was resurrected from the dead. He is exalted in heaven, and has promised to return. Meanwhile the "chosen-ness" of His Jewish family continues to elicit deep inter-family and Gentile resentment. The spirit of anti-Semitism is threatening to become as dangerous today as it was in the time of Persia's Haman or Germany's Hitler.

The Messiah's unique claim to be the very Son of God is as deeply resented and denied today as it was during His Incarnation. People can allow Him to be a teacher or a prophet, but most reject Him as the Son of God. Yet it is His identity as the Son sent by the Father that is the basis of His qualification to be the Father's supreme messenger and the world's only Savior.

Substantiation of His Son-ship from Jesus Himself:

Who did *Yeshua* know Himself to be?   John 5:16-23
What unique relationship to the Father did Jesus proclaim? John 6:46

In what relationship to Abraham did *Yeshua* claim to be?
John 8:54-59

What intimate Father/Son relationship did He reveal to His disciples? John 14:9-11

At His trial, what three identities did *Yeshua* claim?
Matthew 26:63-64

♥ *How crucial do I see His Son-ship to be?*

LAMB (Sacrifice)

Today, something new is challenging the status quo. The number of Jewish believers in *Yeshua* as the true Messiah is mushrooming. They are speaking out. For example, recently they have created materials to expose people in New York and Israel to the message of Isaiah 53. This initiative has opened up an Old Testament chapter forbidden among some Jewish communities. Isaiah 53's clear foreshadowing of the coming Messiah's rejection and crucifixion during His mission as the Lamb of God is hard to deny. Isaiah 53 has deep connections in both Testaments.

Compare Isaiah chapter 53 with New Testament fulfillments.

➢ Isaiah 53:1 "Who has believed..?" - John 1:10-11

➢ Isaiah 53:4 "he took up our infirmities"- Matthew 8:16-17

➢ Isaiah 53:7 "he did not open his mouth"- Matthew 27:12-14

➢ Isaiah 53:7 "led like a lamb to slaughter"- Revelation 5:9-12

➢ Isaiah 53:11 "the suffering of his soul" - Luke 24:25-27

➢ Isaiah 53:12 "poured out his life unto death" - Acts 3:17-18

➢ Isaiah 53:12 "bore the sins of many" - Hebrews 9:11-15

➢ Isaiah 53:22-25 "committed no sin" - I Peter 2:21-25

➢ Isaiah 53:37 "numbered with transgressors"- Luke 22:37

♥ *Do I see His suffering as in my place?*

TWO (Relationships)

We are seeing a transformation take place in recent decades as the "olive tree" is beginning to bud again. Jewish believers are proclaiming *Yeshua's* Messiahship. The inseparability of the two Covenants is being increasingly demonstrated by recently published Jewish translations, such as the *Complete Jewish Bible,* and *the Tree of Life Bible.*

The unexpected rise of the Messianic movement today faces both Israel and the Church with a largely unwelcome reality. The failure of the Reformation in the 1500's to correct false doctrine regarding Israel is having to be re-evaluated. That the Church has *replaced* or *superseded* Israel, that the Church since the Incarnation has become the "new Israel," is still implied implicitly and occasionally taught explicitly in many branches of Christendom. Replacement Theology has influenced Christendom's attitude toward the "root" throughout AD history. Its falseness is slowly being uncovered and confessed by Gentile believers. Reconciliation is afoot. Israel's firm place in God's purposes is being re-considered by thoughtful Christian scholars. *(See the Appendix for examples.)*

The Old Testament gives many assurances of God's unfailing love for Israel, and promises her future restoration. What are some New Testament examples of Israel's continuing role?

Consider these:

> ➢ Matthew 19:28

> ➢ Romans 11:11-26

> ➢ Hebrews 8:6-12

> ➢ Revelation 7:3-8; 14:1-5

> ➢ Revelation 21:2, 9-14

♥ *What is my background on the "Replacement" issue? My view now?*

PRIEST (Mediator)

The Letter to the Hebrews (written while the Temple was still Israel's center of worship) explains the New Covenant believers' relationship to the Temple in the 1st Century. Temple worship soon ceased due to Jerusalem's destruction in 70 AD — just as the final Lamb of God had predicted. Since the Messiah has finished the work of redemption, believers in the Lamb are invited to come boldly to heaven's Throne of Grace (Hebrews 4:16). There our Great High Priest continues to advocate for His people (Hebrews 7:25). When history as we know it comes to its conclusion, He is to eventually come forth from heaven's Holy of Holies. When ancient Israel's Great High Priest emerged on the Day of Atonement, the community breathed a sigh of relief that the atoning blood had been accepted. Our Great High Priest will return from the true Tabernacle as promised.

Having come first to be the sacrificial Lamb of God, for what purpose will He appear on earth the second time?
Hebrews 9:23-28

Where does Scripture describe the glorified Messiah dressed like the Great High Priest? Revelation 1:12-16

♥ *How does Jesus' present ministry as my Great High Priest impact my prayer life?*

HOST (Timing)

The *Torah's* seven Feasts unto the Lord provide clues to God's timing throughout history. Feasts played a major role in the Messiah's ministry, giving Him unique platforms, audiences, and vehicles for teaching. His life, death, and enthronement have already fulfilled the first four Feasts.

Replacement Theology has caused much of the Christian world to lose the Church's connection with the Jewish roots in which the Feasts play such a major role. Few church attenders give serious attention to the *Torah's* teachings that include dozens of chapters focused on the Tabernacle and Feasts. Some Christians have declared all this to have been fulfilled in the 1st Century, cutting their adherents off from a rich vein of meaning and eschatological information.

Those today who are awake to the meaning of the Feasts stand on tiptoe in light of Jesus' commands to His people to watch, to expect His return, and to be prepared. Each fall season alert believers anticipate the possible arrival of the uncompleted Fall Feasts: the Trumpet's call, the return of the Great High Priest on the Day of Atonement, and the Ingathering of the Redeemed.

Just like Jesus' disciples, we too keep asking, "When?" *Yeshua* answered that only the Father knows when. However the Son — the Host of the Feasts — revealed what to expect before His coming. The Spirit gave the disciples further insights that are recorded in the New Testament.

Consider these timing clues from the Lord Jesus and the Apostles:

> ➢ Luke 21:20-24
> ➢ Luke 21:25-36
> ➢ Luke 22:17-18
> ➢ Matthew 24:14
> ➢ Romans 11:25-27
> ➢ I Thessalonians 4:13-18
> ➢ II Peter 3:2-13

♥ *How does the prospect of His imminent return actually affect my daily life?*

KING (Lordship)

Except for captivating epics like Tolkien's "Lord of the Rings" trilogy, the term "king" or "kingdom" is not popular in our age of parliamentary government and democracy. As Christians mouth the liturgical Lord's Prayer, "thy Kingdom come" (in the sense of His bringing in His Kingdom) may be less in mind than human attempts to reform the kingdoms of this world.

Jerusalem, "city of the King," is still the fulcrum of the world's struggles. Israel is confined in a small slice of land about the size of New Jersey. Her flag bravely displays the Star of David. *Yeshua* was rejected in Jerusalem and was crucified as "the king of the Jews" at the climax of the Incarnation. Weeping over Jerusalem's rejection just before the Cross, He prophesied, "Look, your house is left to you desolate. For I tell you, you will not see me again until you say, 'Blessed is he who comes in the name of the Lord.' " The fickle crowd chanted that line out of Psalm 118 during *Yeshua's* supposedly triumphal entry.

What might it mean that today Messianic believers worldwide, notably in Israel, are pouring out songs of real praise quoting Psalm 118? Many individuals and congregations in Israel are earnestly worshiping *Yeshua* as their Messiah as they sing, "Blessed is he who comes in the name of the Lord." *After twenty centuries, is the Messianic community's rebirth a sign of Israel's "olive tree" budding with new life? If so, what might be a Godly response from the Church?*

Consider Paul's warnings and predictions: Romans 11:13-21, 25

Check some of Scripture's Davidic Kingdom-related revelations:
II Samuel 7:11-17

Psalm 89:3-4

Matthew 1:1, 17-18

Luke 1:31-33

John 18:33-37

Acts 1:6-8

Revelation 19:11-16

Revelation 22:16

♥ *What is my response, my personal connection to the Messiah's Kingship?*

PROPHET (Revelation)

Never more urgent are prophecies about the Last Days than in the generation into which one is born! The urgency has been dulled by Replacement Theology which tends to avoid this focus or insist that most prophecies are already fulfilled, or that they are largely metaphorical. The Old Covenant prophets often warned Israel about impending judgment, but also gave hope of eventual restoration. Isaiah 51:1-12, Jeremiah 31:1-14, Ezekiel 37, and Amos 9:11-15 are examples. Their prophecies also foresaw a future time of final return and restoration, an ultimate renewal that Israel has not yet experienced. In Daniel 12:1-4, the angel Michael tells Daniel that his people will be delivered, but the scroll is to be sealed "until the time of the end."

Yeshua, **the ultimate Prophet of the New Covenant,** provided striking descriptions of what to expect at the time of His coming. He kept warning His disciples to be awake, watching, faithful, and enduring, so that they might be overcomers. The kind of signs He warned about are converging rapidly in our generation in compounding and inter-related arenas — political, ecological, geographical, societal, ethical, economic, religious, and more. These kinds of chaos have occurred across the world before, but many are noticing a globalized and cascading scale.

Write down what manifestations we are to expect from Yeshua's predictions cross-referenced in a full chapter of each of three Gospels:
Matthew 24, Mark 13, and Luke 21

What did the risen Christ later command and predict?
Luke 24:36-49

Acts 1:1-8

BRIDEGROOM (Future Consummation)

Leaving our consideration of today's relationship to the Messiah's Old Testament roles, let us look now at the new role revealed in the book of Revelation. We remember that in Old Covenant times, Israel was referred to as the unfaithful "wife." The book of Hosea particularly uses that metaphor. Who is the Church (all Jew and Gentile believers) called as the Bible closes? She is referred to as the "bride"! Marriage customs in the Jewish culture are helpful to understand when we read *Yeshua's* explanation that He would be going to prepare a place for them (John 14:2-3), or when he said that only the Father knew His return's timing (Matthew 24:36). In those days sons built their new home onto the father's house, and the father decided when the wedding would take place.

Although she — the Bride, the Church — also has failed to be faithful, her loving Lord has provided for her to be perfected by the indwelling of the very Spirit of God whom He sent to earth since Pentecost to care for her. Acts 2:33 records this, as John 7:39 explains.

The Bible draws to a close with the Marriage Supper of the Lamb being announced and the Bridegroom's promise to come for the Bride "soon." As we look back to His Incarnation, we find this union was all along on the Son's heart. It was predicted in veiled ways.

What is revealed in each of these Bridegroom "code language" passages?
John 3:27-30

Matthew 9:14-15, Mark 2:19-20, Luke 5:33-34
(cross references)

Matthew 25:1-13

Today's members of the true Bride of Christ wait for His return with eager anticipation, calling out, "Come, Lord Jesus!" (See Revelation 22:17.) He promises lovingly, "Yes, I am coming soon!" Their Wedding Banquet is foreseen. (See Revelation 19:7-8.) Meanwhile, the Bride is being gathered, perfected, and beautified by her ongoing sanctification, purification, suffering, and response to His love.

What does "the blessed hope" mean for today's people of God? The word "hope" often implies uncertainty. Biblical "hope" has been summarized by someone as "the interval between God's promise and His fulfillment." Timing is secondary. God's trustworthiness is primary. If God promises, He fulfills. Our hope is certain.

Will final union with the Bridegroom be worth the wait? May we realize that amazingly, He has been waiting these many centuries, valuing His Bride enough to die for her, and waiting for her responding love. Barely aware of her worth to Him, how awesome will be the Day when she weds and experiences her destiny to share the Throne with Creation's rightful King! In the last chapter of the Bible, He leaves His Bride with a ten-fold description of Himself — the Beloved whose magnificence and sacrificial love is worth waiting for.

Write down His self-revelations and try to imagine marriage with such a Bridegroom:

Revelation 22:12, 16

♥ *Have I personally chosen to BE within the Bride? If so, then how am I purposefully allowing Him to prepare me for this unique wedding to the King of the universe, for our new queenly identity, and for our amazing new life?*

A prayer of assurance for the Bride in I Thessalonians 5:23-24:

May God himself, the God of peace, sanctify you through and through. May your whole spirit, soul and body be kept blameless at the coming of our Lord Jesus Christ. The one who calls you is faithful and he will do it.

Ω

Hold on to the BRIDEGROOM KEY to both Covenants!

Behold I am coming soon. My reward is with me, and I will give to everyone according to what he has done. I am the Alpha and Omega, the First and the Last, the Beginning and the End.

Revelation 22:12-13

APPENDIX

A. Tools for Conserving my Study

♥ *My self evaluation:*

How can I make the most of my time invested in this experience on the Emmaus Road with the risen Messiah?

> The wise evaluate. Webster defines "to evaluate" as "to determine significance or worth by careful appraisal and study." Here are some ways to make your personal *ALL* appraisal in terms of your own integration, conservation, and implementation:

Integration questions:

Having studied eight roles of the Messiah reflected throughout the Bible, am I appreciating or loving Jesus more? In what ways?

....
....
....

Am I finding that my ongoing Bible study has more depth? Specific examples?

....
....
....

Has this study altered my sense of relationship with the Body of Christ, my local church, or my Jewish or Gentile fellow pilgrims? Examples?

....
....
....

How has it changed my view of my own identity, my goals, my destiny, or my fellow pilgrims? Examples?

....

....

....

Spiritual conservation tips:

☞ Memorize SCRIPTURE KEYS for holding on to portrayals of the roles of the Messiah. Use the MESSIANIC GEM VISUAL to picture a summary of our Lord's roles. (The compiled Key Scriptures and the Messianic Gem Visual follow in the Appendix.)

Ω As you study the WORD OF GOD, keep deepening your grasp of the fullness of the Messiah woven throughout the whole Bible. Write cross references in your margins. They can inform each other powerfully.

Implementation opportunities:

→ Go on to study *IN* which will weave the threads the other direction from the New Testament to the Old, and focus on the believer's key to life IN Christ.

⌂ Lead an *ALL* or *IN* study group. Helping others learn is one of the best ways to digest the word of God and let the Spirit make it operational in your own life, as you labor to bring others to maturity.

MM If you are willing to undertake a longer study, consider *The Messiah Mystery*. It parallels the *ALL* and *IN* themes, but includes more detail (300 plus pages) and more reference material. A companion booklet, *Keys to the Messiah Mystery*, is a collection of teaching materials and suggested formats for this panoramic method of study. *The Messiah Mystery's* 24 chapters are also available from the author in Power Point visual form.

B. KEYS TO ALL THE MESSIAH IS

SEED

For since death came through a man, the resurrection from the dead comes also through a man. For as in Adam all die, so in Christ all will be made alive.

I Corinthians 15:21-22

SON

By faith Abraham, when God tested him, offered Isaac as a sacrifice. He who had received the promises was about to sacrifice his one and only son, even though God had said to him, "It is through Isaac that your offspring will be reckoned." Abraham reasoned that God could raise the dead, and figuratively speaking, he did receive Isaac back from death.

Hebrews 11:17-19

LAMB

The next day John saw Jesus coming toward him and said, "Look, the Lamb of God, who takes away the sin of the world!"

John 1:29

PRIEST

When Christ came as high priest of the good things that are already here, he went through the greater and more perfect tabernacle that is not man-made, that is to say, not a part of this creation. He did not enter by means of the blood of goats and calves; but he entered the Most Holy Place once for all by his own blood, having obtained eternal redemption.

Hebrews 9:11-12

HOST

For Christ our Passover lamb has been sacrificed. Therefore let us keep the Festival, not with the old yeast, the yeast of malice and wickedness, but with bread without yeast, the bread of sincerity and truth.

I Corinthians 5:7b-8

KING

"I, Jesus, have sent my angel to give you this testimony for the churches. I am the Root and the Offspring of David, and the bright Morning Star."

Revelation 22:16

PROPHET

In the past God spoke to our forefathers through the prophets at many times and in various ways, but in these last days he has spoken to us by his son, through whom he made the universe.

Hebrews 1:1-2

ALL

He said to them, "how foolish you are, and how slow [of heart] to believe all that the prophets have spoken! Did not the Messiah have to suffer these things and then enter his glory?" And beginning with Moses and all the Prophets, he explained to them what was said in all the Scriptures concerning himself.

Luke 24:25-27 (NIV 2011)

C. THE MESSIANIC GEM VISUAL
ALL: Luke 24:25-27

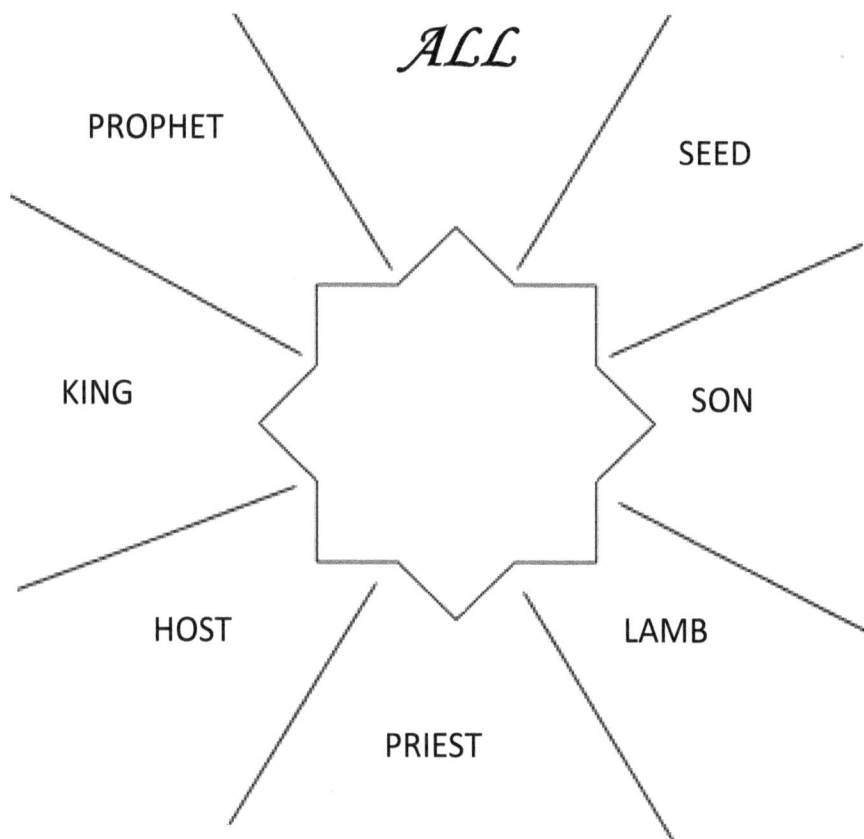

ALL

PROPHET

SEED

KING

SON

HOST

LAMB

PRIEST

THE MESSIAH'S
OLD COVENANT ROLES
PICTURED AS
FACETS OF THE MESSIANIC GEM

Read from 1:00 clockwise, moving through "Moses and the prophets" – the Old Testament – from Genesis to Malachi. Correlate the Gem Illustration above with Appendix B Key Verses. Together they demonstrate the Old and New Testaments' inseparable disclosure.

BIBLIOGRAPHY

Edersheim, Alfred, *The Life and Times of Jesus the Messiah,* Oxford, l886, reprinted by Eerdmans, Grand Rapids, Michigan, 1976.

Jones, E. Stanley, *The Word Became Flesh*, Abingdon Press, Nashville, Tennessee, l963.

Nee, Watchman, *The Normal Christian Life*, Christian Literature Crusade, Fort Washington, Pennsylvania, paperback edition, reprinted in 1965.

Stern, David H., *The Complete Jewish Bible*, Jewish New Testament Publications, Clarksville, Maryland, Jerusalem, Israel, l998.

Tolkien, J. R. R., *The Lord of the Rings* Part III, *The Return of the King*, Ballentine Books, New York, 1994.

Tree of Life (TLV) Translation of the Bible, The Messianic Jewish Family Bible Society, Rome, Georgia, 2015.

Resources on the Law, Priesthood, Tabernacle, Temple, and Feasts:

Edersheim, Alfred, *The Life and Times of Jesus the Messiah,* Oxford, l886, reprinted by Eerdmans, Grand Rapids, Michigan, 1976.

Mackintosh, C.H., *Genesis to Deuteronomy*, Loizeaux Brothers, Neptune, New Jersey, l972.

Rose Publishing resources - 5 ½ x 8 ½ open out panels and larger wall charts, including ones on the Tabernacle, Temple, and Feasts. www.rose-publishing.com, Torrance, California, 2005 and other publishing dates.

Rosen, Ceil and Moishe, *Christ in the Passover*, Moody Press, Chicago, 1978.

Solteau, Henry William, *The Tabernacle*, Kregel Publications, Grand Rapids, Michigan, reprinted l971.

Zimmerman, Martha, *Celebrating the Biblical Feasts,* Bethany House Publishers, Ada, Michigan, 2004.

Resources on the Messianic Movement, and Jewish/Church Relationships:

Brown, Michael L., *Our Hands are Stained with Blood*, Destiny Image Publishers, Shippensburg, PA, 1992.

Gundry, Stanley N., Series Editor, *How Jewish is Christianity?* Zondervan, Grand Rapids, Michigan, 2003.

Horner, Barry E, *Future Israel: Why Christian Anti-Judaism Must Be Challenged*, B&H Publishing Group, Nashville, Tennessee, 2007.

Jocz, Jakob, *The Jewish People and Jesus Christ after Auschwitz*, Baker Book House, Grand Rapids, Michigan, 1981.

Liberman, Paul, and Wasson, Jack, *Don't Call Me Christian: A Truly Jewish Story*, Tishbite Press, Arlington, TX, 2015.

McQuaid, Elwood, *The Zion Connection*, Harvest House Publishers, Eugene, Oregon, 1996.

Stern, David H., *Messianic Jewish Manifesto*, Jewish New Testament Publications, Jerusalem, Israel, 1988. [It has since been re-published as *Messianic Judaism: A Modern Movement with an Ancient Past*, Messianic Jewish Publishers, Clarksville, Maryland, 2007.]

Stern, David H., *Restoring the Jewishness of the Gospel*, Jewish New Testament Publications, Jerusalem, Israel, 1988.

Stern, David H., *The Complete Jewish Bible*, Jewish New Testament Publications, Clarksville, Maryland, Jerusalem, Israel, 1998.

Telchin, Stan, *Betrayed*, Chosen Books, Ada, Michigan, 2007.

Vlach, Michael J., *Has the Church Replaced Israel?* B&H Publishing Group, Nashville, Tennessee, 2010.

Wilson, Marvin R., *Our Father Abraham*, Wm B. Eerdmans Publishing Company, Grand Rapids, MI, 1989.

To contact the author:

charlesnkbascom@gmail.com

The author's website:

www.messiahmysteryresources.org

$\mathcal{ALL}$

is available at:

olivepresspublisher.com

amazon.com

barnesandnoble.com

christianbook.com

and other online stores

Store managers:

Order wholesale through:

Ingram Book Company or

Spring Arbor

or by emailing:

olivepressbooks@gmail.com